POLICE CORRUPTION

An Empirical Typology of

POLICE

CORRUPTION

A Study in Organizational Deviance

By

THOMAS BARKER, M.A.
National Defense Educational Act Fellow

and

JULIAN ROEBUCK, Ph.D.
Professor of Sociology
Mississippi State University
Mississippi State, Mississippi

CHARLES C THOMAS · PUBLISHER
Springfield · Illinois · U.S.A.

Published and Distributed Throughout the World by
CHARLES C THOMAS · PUBLISHER
BANNERSTONE HOUSE
301-327 East Lawrence Avenue, Springfield, Illinois, U.S.A.

Library of Congress Cataloging in Publication Data

Barker, Thomas.
    An empirical typology of police corruption.

    1. Police corruption.   I. Roebuck, Julian B.,
joint author.   II. Title.
HV7935.B37   364-1'32   73-8525
ISBN 0-398-02896-6

Printed in the United States of America
H-1

To

ELIZABETH JANE FINN BARKER
and
MARYBETH LOUISE ROEBUCK

PREFACE

THIS MANUSCRIPT develops an empirical typology of police corruption derived from a content analysis of literature (1960-1972) and the police work experience of one of the writers. Police corruption is analyzed, not as the exclusive deviant behavior of a few *rotten apples,* but as a form of organizational deviance hinging primarily on informal police peer group norms. Contradictions among formal norms, informal norms, and situational rules are indicated. Eight types of police corruption are delineated: (1) Corruption of Authority, (2) Kickbacks, (3) Opportunistic Theft: From Arrestees, Victims, Crime Scenes, and Unprotected Property, (4) Shakedowns, (5) Protection of Illegal Activities, (6) The Fix, (7) Direct Criminal Activities, and (8) Internal Payoffs. The types are analyzed along several dimensions: (1) Acts and actors, (2) norm violations, (3) support from peer group, (4) organizational degree of deviant practices, and (5) police department's reactions.

The suggested dynamic typology along with a four-step implementation method represents a triangular methodology; i.e. a series of common data bases; a reliable sampling model that recognizes interaction; a series of empirical indicators for each data base; and a series of testable conceptualizations.

This manuscript is directed to criminologists, students of deviant behavior, political scientists, academicians and all those interested in the administration of criminal justice, especially law enforcement personnel and those responsible for police policy and its implementation. It may be used as supplementary class material in criminology, police science, deviant behavior, and social problems courses. Certainly concerned layman will be interested in its substantive materials.

THOMAS BARKER
JULIAN B. ROEBUCK

CONTENTS

POLICE CORRUPTION

POLICE CORRUPTION

CHAPTER I

REVIEW OF LITERATURE AND PROBLEM STATEMENT

INTRODUCTION

POLICE CORRUPTION is a topic of universal and persistent concern for many Americans. However, there is no uniform agreement about its definition or boundaries. Police corruption is loosely identified in the literature as deviant, dishonest, improper, unethical or criminal behavior by a police officer. Its delineation is difficult because of the ambiguity of the policeman's role in the dynamic and heterogeneous American society. Police role ambiguity confuses the distinction be-tween proper and improper police conduct.[1] Many citizens, as in-dividuals and as members of special interest groups (varying from special pleaders for strict law and order to avid advocates of the pro-tection of civil liberties), express conflicting feelings and ideas about this field of deviant behavior. Scholars, politicians, journalists, muck-rakers, reformers, writers, newscasters, and intellectuals of variegated persuasions enunciate a melange of views about police corruption and its causation.[2]

---

[1] For a discussion of police role ambiguity see O. W. Wilson, "Police Authority in a Free Society," *Journal of Criminal Law, Criminology and Police Science*, 54: 175-177, (June, 1963); J. McIntyre, "Public Attitudes Toward Crime and Law Enforcement," *Annals of the American Academy of Political and Social Science*, 370: 34-36 (Nov. 1967); R. D. Knudten, *Crime Criminology and Contemporary Society* (Homewood, 1970), pp. 203-205; W. Dienstein, "Sociology of Law En-forcement," In *Crime Criminology and Contemporary Society*, (Ed.) R. D. Knudten, pp. 205-211; E. Cumming, I. Cumming, and L. Edell, "Policeman as Philosopher, Guide and Friend," In *Crime, Criminology and Contemporary Soci-ety*, pp. 211-212; E. Bittner, *The Functions of the Police in Modern Society: A Review of Background Factors, Current Practices and Possible Role Models* (Washington, D. C., U. S. Dept. of Health, Education and Welfare, Pub. No. (HSM) 72-9103, 1972).

[2] For a discussion of police deviancy and illegal behavior, including a review of the literature, see E. R. Stoddard, " 'The Informal Code' of Police Deviancy: A

Behavioral scientists have not made a systematic study of this phenomenon which occurs within a diverse assortment of law enforcement agencies. One reason is the neglect by criminologists of law enforcement agencies. Until recently police systems were made inaccessible to social scientists. It is now fashionable for criminologists to study law enforcement establishments. Police administrators concerned with professionalizing their departments have begun to realize the benefits of collaborative research with social scientists. Sociologists, who have investigated law enforcement agencies, have concentrated their efforts in three areas: occupational issues in performance of the police role, police system organization and police-community relations.[3] Police corruption has been dealt with only tangentially. In fact, one sociologist states he avoided police corruption in his research because the subject was *to hot to handle*.[4]

REVIEW OF THE LITERATURE

The vast content of the literature deals with value laden accounts by muckraking journalists and the confessions of exposed police officers.[5] The few articles and selections appearing in scholarly journals and books are based on case study methods of ex-officer's confessions about criminal activities.[6] Criminology and police text materials

---

Group Approach to 'Blue Coat Crime,' " *Journal of Criminal Law, Criminology and Police Science,* 59: 201-213 (June, 1968). For group support of police violence and misconduct see W. A. Westley, *Violence and the Police: A Sociological Study of Law, Custom and Morality* (Cambridge, 1970), pp. 15-48, 109-153. For a lack of substance delineation and precise theoretical conceptualization within the area of police corruption see The President's Commission on Law Enforcement and Administration of Justice, *Task Force Report: The Police* (Washington, D. C., 1967), pp. 208-215.

[3] A. L. Guenther, (Ed.), "Control Systems 1: The Police and Law Enforcement," *Criminal Behavior and Social Systems* (Chicago, 1970), pp. 311-315.

[4] W. A. Westley, *Violence and the Police,* p. 201.

[5] Examples of such works are David C. Wittels, "Why Cops Turn Crooked," *Saturday Evening Post,* April 23, 1949, pp. 26-27, 104-109, 111, 114-122; Albert Deutch, *The Trouble With Cops* (New York, 1955); Ralph L. Smith, *The Tarnished Badge* (New York, 1965); Hank Messick, *Syndicate in the Sun* (New York, 1968); Ted Poston, "The Numbers Racket," in F. R. Cressey and D. A. Ward, eds., *Delinquency, Crime and Social Process* (New York, 1969), pp. 920-934; W. T. Brannon, *The Crooked Cops* (Chicago, 1962).

[6] Mort Stern, "What Makes a Policeman Go Wrong?" *Journal of Criminal Law, Criminology and Police Science,* 52: 98-101 (March, 1962); Ellwyn R. Stoddard, "The Informal Code of Police Deviancy."

in a cursory and descriptive manner deal with lawless and corrupt police, e.g. graft, collusion with criminals and crooked politicians, and bribery.[7] Deviant behavior books offer no specific selections on police corruption. Behavioral scientists, who have engaged in the participant observation of the police, have paid scant attention to police corruption *per se,* although several have furnished sketchy accounts.[8]

Many social scientists, who have mentioned this subject in their writings, have offered (seemingly) plausible accounts for the existence of corrupt police behavior ranging from extreme individualistic postulates to cultural determinism: personality aberrations,[9] dishonest and criminal recruits,[10] faulty training and supervision,[11] low pay and occupational status,[12] political corruption,[13] type and orientation of police organization,[14] weak leadership in the community and the

---

[7] For textbook coverage see Walter C. Reckless, *The Crime Problem* (New York, 1967), pp. 279-319; Don C. Gibbons, *Society Crime and Criminal Careers* (Englewood Cliffs, 1968), pp. 47-70, Edwin H. Sutherland and Donald R. Cressey, *Criminology* 8th ed. (Philadelphia, 1970), pp. 374-400. For historical accounts of police corruption see Frank Tannenbaum, *Crime and the Community* (Boston, 1938); Estes Kefauver and others, *Third Interim Report of the Special Committee to Investigate Organized Crime in Gambling and Racketeering Activities,* Report No. 307 (Washington, D. C., 1951); Gus Tyler, *Organized Crime in America* (Ann Arbor, 1962); John Kobler, *Capone: The Life and World of Al Capone* (New York, 1971); Charles Winick and Paul M. Kinsie, *The Lively Commerce: Prostitution in the United States* (Chicago, 1971), pp. 103, 214, 241. For more recent accounts see James Q. Wilson, *Varieties of Police Behavior* (New York, 1970); Leon Radzinowicz and Marvin E. Wolfgang, eds., *Crime and Justice Vol. II, The Criminal in the Arms of the Law, Part II, The Police* (New York, 1971), pp. 147-362; Ralph Salerno and John S. Tomkins, *The Crime Confederation* (New York, 1969); Albert J. Reiss Jr., *The Police and the Public* (New Haven, 1972), pp. 121-173.

[8] Examples of such works are Egon Bittner, "The Police on Skid Row: A Study of Peace Keeping," *American Sociological Review,* 32:699-715 (October, 1967); Jerome H. Skolnick, *Justice Without Trial: Law Enforcement in Democratic Society* (New York, 1971); and William A. Westley, *Violence and the Police.*

[9] Theodore Kemper, "Representative Roles and Legitimation of Deviance," *Social Problems,* 13: 288-298 (1966).

[10] Earl B. Lewis and Richard Blum, eds., "Selection Standards: A Critical Approach," *Police Selection* (Springfield, 1964), p. 54.

[11] Paul W. Tappan, *Crime, Justice and Correction* (New York, 1960), pp. 309-313.

[12] Elmer H. Johnson, *Crime, Correction and Society* (Homewood, 1964), p. 452.

[13] John A. Gardiner, *The Politics of Corruption* (New York, 1970).

[14] Edward Robert Mitchell, "Organization as a Key to Police Effectiveness," *Crime and Delinquency,* 12: 344-352 (1966); James Q. Wilson, *Varieties of Police Behavior,* pp. 140-200.

police department,[15] dearth of professional standards in police organizations,[16] community social structure and criminal and corrupt tolerance limits,[17] functional consequence of societal demands for illegal services, [18] concomitant result of the Volstead Act,[19] consonant behavior with crime as an American way of life,[20] police role conflicts in a democracy,[21] and socialization of new recruits into corrupt police code participation.[22] However, none of these explanations represent systematic theory supported by empirical research.

PROBLEM STATEMENT

The primary problem in the study of police corruption is a lack of substance delineation, classification and articulation. The purpose of this book is to develop an empirical typology of police corruption utilizable in field research.[23] First, dimensions of study within specific theoretical frames of reference are designated. Then, the extended, amorphous area of police corruption, diverging from the acceptance of gifts and gratuities to direct criminal activities, is broken down into more homogeneous, patterned units of study. The dimensions of study are used to analyze these unitary types. Lastly,

---

[15] John E. Ingersoll, "The Police Scandal Syndrome: Conditions Leading to an Apparent Breakdown in Police Service," *Crime and Delinquency, 10*: 296-275, (July, 1964).

[16] Jerome H. Skolnick, *Justice Without Trial*, pp. 256-258.

[17] James Q. Wilson, *Varieties of Police Behavior*, pp. 99-103.

[18] William F. Whyte Jr., *Street Corner Society* (Chicago, 1955), pp. 138-139; Richard R. Korn and Lloyd W. McCorkel, *Criminology and Penology* (New York, 1959), pp. 85-86; Robert K. Merton, *Social Theory and Social Structure* (New York, 1958), pp. 19-82, 121-159, 161-192; Walter C. Reckless, *The Crime Problem*, pp. 335-343; Edwin M. Schur, *Our Criminal Society: The Social and Legal Sources of Crime in America* (Englewood Cliffs, N. J., 1969), p. 200.

[19] Ralph Salerno and John S. Tomkins, *The Crime Confederation* (Garden City), p. 279.

[20] Daniel Bell, *The End of Ideology* (New York, 1960), pp. 115-136.

[21] Jerome H. Skolnick, *Justice Without Trial*, pp. 1-17.

[22] Ellwyn R. Stoddard, "The Informal Code of Police Deviancy."

[23] The guidelines for the construction of a typology are discussed in Theodore Ferdinand, *Typologies of Delinquency: A Critical Analysis* (New York, 1966), pp. 41-71; Don C. Gibbons, *Changing the Lawbreaker* (Englewood Cliffs, N. J., 1965), pp. 74-120; and Marshall B. Clinard and Richard Quinney, *Criminal Behavior Systems, A Typology* (New York, 1967), pp. 1-19. See also Carl H. Hempel, "Symposium: Problems of Concept and Theory Formation in the Social Sciences," *Science, Language and Human Rights,* I (Philadelphia, 1952), 65-80.

a triangular methodology is proposed for the typology's implementation. The foregoing steps are prerequisite to further explanatory theory, the understanding of police corruption as social process and as *functional* or *dysfunctional* behavior.

CHAPTER II

DEFINITION OF CONCEPTS AND THEORETICAL ORIENTATION

INTRODUCTION

INFORMAL PRACTICES within police departments may often be highly formalized. They may be written down. Formal written departmental policy and procedure may be considered informal with respect to the law. Operating norms at all levels in police organizations may differ from either the law or departmental written rules. Therefore, in order to arrive at the difficult task of defining police corruption, it is necessary to recognize the problematic and contradictory definitions of police organizational norms.[24] Any analysis of corrupt police behavior must include three levels of (definitional) analysis: (1) formal norms (publicly avowed), (2) informal (operating) norms, and (3) problematic situational social meanings or rules which arise within a law enforcement officer's occupational milieu.

DEFINITIONS OF CONCEPTS AND METHODOLOGY

Police corruption is operationally defined as any type of *prescribed* behavior engaged in by a law enforcement officer who receives or expects to receive, by virtue of his official position, an actual or poten-

---

[24] For a discussion and analysis of these conflicting and problematic norms see Joseph Goldstein, "Police Discretion Not to Invoke the Criminal Process: Low-Visibility Decisions in the Administration of Criminal Justice," *Yale Law Journal,* 64: 543-594 (March, 1960); John H. McNamara, "Uncertainties in Police Work: The Relevance of Police Recruits Background and Training," in Bordua, David J. (ed.), *The Police; Six Sociological Essays* (New York, 1967) pp. 163-252; Albert J. Reiss Jr., and David J. Bordua, "Environment and Organization: A Perspective on the Police," in *The Police: Six Sociological Essays,* pp. 320-322; Bernard Cohen, "The Police Internal System of Justice in New York City," *Journal of Criminal Law, Criminology and Police Science,* LXIII (March 1972), 54-68 (March 1972).

tial *unauthorized* material reward or gain. Behaviors, defined as police corruption transgress normative systems:[25] (1) violations of formal (written) police departmental administrative rules, laws, regulations, policies; (2) violations of informal (general operating) rules; (3) violations of criminal laws. Obviously from either a theoretical or applied sense, contradictions will exist in any classification system utilizing these three categories.

Transgressions of norms prescribed by a law enforcement officer's sworn oath of office and/or other formal norms are not always violations of criminal laws, but all violations of criminal laws are violations of an officer's sworn oath of office and/or other formal norms. Informal rules (governing informal practices) may or may not violate formal or legal norms; i.e. they may be in contradiction with one or the other or both. Violations may vary, then, from transgressions of prescribed ethical conduct to engagement in criminal activities.[26]

The operational definition utilized in the construction of a typology

[25] The normative systems approach has its limitations because social rules have problematic meanings. Moreover, policemen, as well as others, construct their meanings of social rules from several sources: abstract meanings, informal meanings, social situational meanings, symbolic meanings brought to the situation by the actor-including morality and past socialization. See Jack D. Douglas, *American Social Order* (New York, 1971), pp. 171-243.

[26] The Code of Ethics adopted by the International Association of Chiefs of Police prescribes police ethical conduct:

> . . . I will never act officiously or permit personal feelings, prejudices, animosities, or friendships to influence my decisions. With no compromise for crime and with relentless prosecution of criminals, I will enforce the law courteously and appropriately without fear or favor, malice or ill will, never employing unnecessary force or violence, and never accepting gratuities . . .

in O.W. Wilson, *Police Administration* (New York, 1963), p. 6. Also see The President's Commission on Law Enforcement and Administration of Justice, *Task Force Report: The Police*, p. 213. This commission recommends that all police departments should outline the acceptance of gifts, gratuities and favors by police as unethical.

Goffman notes that Simmel suggested that ethical conduct refers to the informal code sustained by individuals acting in special subworlds wherein only part of the self becomes subject to judgment. Erving Goffman, *Relations in Public* (New York, 1971), p. 97. Therefore, whenever a person willingly becomes a member of a special sub-world, such as a policeman does when he joins a police department and swears to abide by its ethical code, he surrenders a part of his selfhood to scrutiny and sanction by that subworld's ethical code.

of police corruption as deviant behavior is based on (1) the police work experience of the senior author, a seven year veteran with a police department in a standard metropolitan statistical area of over 700,000 people and (2) a content analysis (1960-1972) of the literature on police practices and police corruption. In the examination of recent police work experience, the senior author has used naturalistic inquiry to retrospectfully examine observations of corrupt acts and actors. The typology in form and content reflects this retrospection. Naturalistic inquiry requires the sociologist to treat himself as both object and subject in his studies and record and analyze his behavior as he would any other actor in the interaction process. Basic to this naturalism is the introspective probe of the subjective features of the researchers behavior through an examination of his thoughts at the time of the act. Introspection allows the researcher to record and examine his behavior and the behaviors of others within a sociological framework.[27]

THEORETICAL ORIENTATION

Police corruption is best understood, not as the exclusive deviant behavior of individual officers, but as group behavior guided by contradictory sets of norms linked to the organization to which the erring individuals belong—organizational deviancy.[28] Police corruption is viewed from the deviant behavior approach i.e. deviant behavior is behavior that violates normative expectations.[29] Corrupt acts that are criminal are deviant by definition. Acts proscribed by formal

[27] For a discussion of naturalistic inquiry see Norman K. Denzin, "The Logic of Naturalistic Inquiry," *Social Forces, 50*: 166-182 (December 1971).

[28] For a theoretical discussion of organizational deviance see Albert J. Reiss, Jr., "The Study of Deviant Behavior: Where the Action Is," in Mark Lefton, James K. Skipper Jr., and Charles H. McGaghy (Eds.): *Approaches to Deviance* (New York, 1968) pp. 56-66. Although recognizing the organizational nature of police corruption, the nomenclature of the typology is based on individual policeman's acts, because the courts rarely take judicial notice of written police department rules and decide cases as though the deviating corrupt individual policeman was a free agent. Individual policemen, not police organizations, are cited for illegal and corrupt acts by citizens; police organizations cite individuals, rather than organizational units for illegal and corrupt acts. In short, corrupt police behavior is defined administratively and legally in terms of individual violations. See The President's Commission on Law Enforcement and Administration of Justice, *Task Force Report: The Police*, pp. 28-35.

[29] Earl Rubington and Martin S. Weinberg, *The Study of Social Problems* (New York, 1971), p. 126.

police departmental administrative rules, laws, regulations, and policies (written and unwritten), as well as acts proscribed by informal operating procedures, are also deviant because they transgress norms prescribed by the group to which the law enforcement officer belongs and swears allegiance.

Four linkages illustrate the organizational nature of police corruption, one general and three specific.

First Linkage.—Law enforcement as a subsystem within the legal system of the United States engenders built-in deviant, if not corrupt, police practices endemic to bureaucratic police organization in a democracy. Law enforcement is a subsystem within the legal system including the public prosecutor, legal counsel, the judiciary, and corrections. Nowhere within this legal system is there a formal provision for the organizational subordination of one subsystem to the others so that decisions in any one subsystem can be directly and effectively enforced in others by administrative or other organizational sanctions. These subsystems are loosely articulated units in the legal system and possess divergent ends. Therefore, conflict (in both internal structure and external relationships) "arises as to the means which each organization may use to achieve its immediate organizational ends, vis-a-vis, those of the legal system, qua legal system."[30]

The courts and the police are institutionally independent and in a relationship of "antagonistic cooperation" so that the legal order can be described only with difficulty as the *client* of the police.[31] The courts are in a position to influence but not control the police. Judges can not maintain a one-sided relationship with the police because the police are a party to matters before the court and they are nearly always on the side of prosecution. If judges were to control the actions of the police, they would then be in a position to determine how police work should be done and, therefore, be responsible for the way it is done. This arrangement would not allow a judge to disinterestedly review the merits of cases presented by the police.[32]

[30] Albert J. Reiss, Jr., and Donald J. Black, "Interrogation and the Criminal Process," *The Annals of the American Academy of Political and Social Science,* *374*: 47-57 (November 1967).

[31] Albert J. Reiss, Jr., and David J. Bordua, "Environment and Organization: A Reflection on the Police," p. 36.

[32] Egon Bittner, *The Functions of the Police in Modern Society,* pp. 31-35.

In many ways, the respect for private ordering that is formal in
civil law is informal in criminal law. Unlike the civil side, a large
body of officials (the police) intervene between law and practice and
may come to participate in such private arrangements themselves.
Informal practice allows the police to vary their relationships, decisions,
and actions within a discretionary frame. Law statutes cannot encompass all the complex circumstances in which they might be applied.
Consequently, the basic responsibility for determining the legal pro-
priety of personal conduct is vested with the police. This informal
discretion is built into legislative acts— e.g. the legislature enacts a
law outlawing all forms of gambling even though they have no inten-
tion of including private games and gambling by non-profit organizations; but to exclude private gambling would allow professional
gamblers to hide behind a facade of privacy. Instead, legislators
presume that the police will exercise discretion in carrying out the law
and therefore, take no action against private gambling and non-profit
organizations. Moreover, the separation of enforcement from out-
come in the American legal system forces the police into a bargain-
ing situation that includes violators, prosecutors, defense attorneys,
courts and correctional personnel.[32]

Finally, a democratic society requires the police to maintain order,
to enforce the law, to protect citizens and property, within a due
process framework i.e. the rule of law. This rule of law is often in-
compatible with the maintenance of law and order, therefore, occupational role conflicts. Furthermore, the recent increase of bureaucratic enabling regulations and the increased efforts to professionalize
police organizations in the United States have logically led to further
discretionary innovations that evoke administrative effciency, but at
the same time operate in opposition to the due process of law.[34] The
police may break the law to enforce the law— e.g. break into businesses
and private dwellings to install electronic surveillance devices, make
illegal harassment arrests, allow fences and bootleggers to operate, tap

---

[33] Albert J. Reiss, Jr., and David J. Bordua, "Environment and Organization:
A Reflection on the Police," pp. 35-40. Herbert A. Bloch and Gilbert Geiss, *Man
Crime and Society: The Forms of Criminal Behavior* (New York, 1962), p. 459;
Harlan Hahn, ed. "The Public and the Police," in *Police in Urban Society*
(Beverly Hills, Calif., 1971).

[34] Jerome H. Skolnick, *Justice Without Trial*, pp. 230-245.

phones, pay-off informers, reduce charges to insure convictions, and underenforce or not enforce certain laws. These acts, when routinized in police practices are readily convertible to personal gain or corrupt practices. This dilemma is probably inescapable in a democracy. The courts are organized to articulate a moral order, a system of values and norms, rather than an order of behavior in public and private places, and the police, by contrast are organized to articulate a behavior system to maintain law and order as bureaucrats and as police officers.[35]

SECOND LINKAGE.—The police organization is often labeled a deviant organization as a consequence of the discovered and labeled behavior of some of its members.[36] Whenever police officers are exposed for engaging in corrupt acts, they receive extensive coverage in the news media. Frequently, this exposure sullies the reputation of the whole organization in that the deviant label is applied to the total membership.

THIRD LINKAGE.—A police organization may support deviant activities of its membership through the use of cover-up tactics.[37] For several reasons, some police organizations are reluctant to expose, label and publicly punish their own members for violations which result in automatic sanction for non-members. Albert Deutsch found the use of cover-up tactics "among law-enforcement officers who are personally untainted by corruption. Personally honest police chiefs will go to extraordinary lengths—even to the point of making fools or suspects of themselves in public—in efforts to shield from exposure crooks and incompetents within the ranks."[38] Sanctioned officers may be secretly tried, warned, or punished, transferred to another departmental unit or assignment, permitted to resign in lieu of dismissal and/or prosecution.[39] These procedures support corrupt

---

[35] Albert J. Reiss, Jr., *The Police and the Public* (New Haven, 1972), p. 117.

[36] Albert J. Reiss, Jr., "The Study of Deviant Behavior," p. 64.

[37] For a discussion of the use of cover-up tactics by organized institutions see Howard S. Becker, *Outsiders: Studies in the Sociology of Deviances* (New York, 1963), pp. 168-169.

[38] Albert Deutsch, *The Trobule With Cops,* pp. 39-40.

[39] William W. Turner, *The Police Establishment* (New York, 1968), p. 34: "To an amazing degree, crimes that would send an ordinary citizen to prison are punishable by mild reprimands, transfers, light suspensions without pay or requests for resignation. Dismissals are rare, and criminal prosecutions ever rarer."

behavior because an officer, after weighing the risk and gain involved in a contemplated proscribed act, might decide that the gain would outweigh the risk of being caught and mildly punished.

Police organizations may use cover-up tactics for organizational, rather than individual protection reasons—e.g. (1) stigma management and (2) corrupt organizational management. In stigma management, the organization realizes that it may be labeled deviant by the deviancy of some of its members and, therefore, handles matters of corruption quietly and secretly in order not to spoil its social identity.[40] On the other hand, a thoroughly deviant police organization (one in which the power structure and/or a number of its members are corrupt) attempts to prevent investigations into its activities through cover-up tactics. Skolnick reports the case of a police organization so corrupt that its members were surprised to find that a nearby city had no police corruption.[41] Many police departments, including those of Chicago and New York City, have utilized cover-up tactics.[42]

FOURTH LINKAGE.—An illustrative fourth link between the organization and the deviancy of its members inheres in the norms and values of the police organiaztion that may covertly support or condone selected deviant police practices. The Commission to Investigate Police Corruption (Knapp Commission) in New York City concluded:

> A fundamental conclusion at which the Commission has arrived is that the problem of police corruption cannot—as is usually asserted—be met by seeking out the few *rotten apples* whose supposedly atypical conduct is claimed to sully the reputation of an otherwise innocent Department. The commission is persuaded that the climate of the department is inhospitable to attempts to uncover acts of corruption, and protective of those who are corrupt. The consequence is that the rookie who comes into the Department is faced with the situation where it is easier for him to become corrupt than to remain honest.[43]

Policeman may witness corrupt police practices on the part of fellow officers (acts they condemn) but fail to report because of either a sense of comradeship with the erring policeman or because of the

---

[40] Erving Goffman, Stigma: *Notes on the Management of Spoiled Identity* (Englewood Cliffs, 1963).

[41] Jerome H. Skolnick, *Justice Without Trial,* pp. 257-258.

[42] William W. Turner, *The Police Establishment,* p. 55.

[43] Commission to Investigate Alleged Police Corruption, *Interim Report on Investigative Phase* (New York, July 1, 1971), p. 2.

organization's norm of secrecy—about *squealing on* or reporting fellow officers for misconduct. Often, in these circumstances, officers will either lie or equivocate about the deviant transaction or claim a lack of knowledge about it. Such fraternal and/or organizational commitments that protect deviants within the group are not uncommon to other associations: in similar ways doctors often protect each other from malpractice suits.

The consistent norms of secrecy inhering in police organizations support police solidarity and simultaneously corruption.[44] August Vollmer remarked a number of years ago that the eradication of police corruption was made difficult because it was next to impossible to persuade police officers to inform on each other. "It is an unwritten law in police departments that police officers must never testify against their brother officers."[45] It is likely that those few officers who testify against another officer do so under extreme duress—e.g. one officer thought to be involved in disclosed proscribed behavior may be given the opportunity to testify in return for leniency with the understanding that should he refuse to talk other suspected officers will be offered the same deal for leniency i.e. a deal for which he will bear the brunt of punishment.

The norm of secrecy is likely to be the first general rule to which the rookie officer is introduced. Often he is considered an outsider and isolated from certain privileged information and situations until (1) he has proven that he can keep his mouth shut and (2) he is *straight, all right, or regular* i.e. he is willing to go along with *what's happening.*

The officer who talks too much is perceived as a threat to everyone. He may reveal mistakes in judgment, personal indiscretions, and violations of departmental or criminal norms. His loose talk can give the department a bad name or bring on an investigation. Therefore,

[44] "Corruption cannot exist without the 'honest' cop. When the honest cop will not inform on his crooked partner, he creates the climate that lets the dishonest cop operate with impunity. . . . No corruption can exist on a widescale basis without fellow officers being aware of it. It is the honest cop who can stop it— but not if he adopts the code of silence and turns his back . . ." Statement made by Joseph Fisch, chief counsel for the New York State Commission of Investigation. Quoted in Fred J. Cook, "The Pusher-Cop: The Institutionalizing of Police Corruption." *New York,* August 16, 1971, p. 30.

[45] William A. Westley, *Violence and the Police,* p. 5.

officers who violate the norm of secrecy are accorded the primary sanction among police, the silent treatment; they are shut off from all sources of information. This leads to untoward consequences for the sanctioned officer because information is essential for an officer's success and protection, e.g. the isolate is unable to learn of criminals active in his area and the nature of informal policies. Also, fellow officers will request not to work with the *isolate* and often will not respond to his calls for assistance.[46]

The support that the deviant officer receives from his peer group may depend upon the consensual and routinized definition of the situation. For example, money taken from those engaged in illegal activities pertaining to gambling, prostitution, and liquor might be defined as *clean money.*[47] Policemen in some departments who take money from these operators may not be defined as deviant, but as "realistic."[48] Some officers rationalize the taking of *clean* money by telling themselves and others that they are responding to a situation forced upon them by the disparity between what is forbidden by law and what is wanted by the community. On the other hand, money received from narcotics pushers and money derived from direct criminal activities such as burglary and robbery are frequently defined as *dirty* money. Police who regularly take *clean* money look down on their colleagues who take *dirty* money as crooks and deviants.

The widespread demand for and traffic in narcotics provide a variety of corrupt opportunities for law enforcement officers, and members of some police departments have begun to accept narcotics pay-offs, which have been traditionally defined as *dirty* money crime. Testimony by police officers to the Knapp Commission includes allegations of wide scale, corrupt police involvement in narcotics traffiking e.g. the acceptance of protection money by police from narcotics dealers, police appropriation and sale of confiscated narcotics.[49]

---

[46] *Ibid.,* pp. 186-187. See also Albert J. Reiss, Jr., *The Police and the Public,* p. 213.

[47] For a discussion of *clean* and *dirty* money by exlaw enforcement officers see William W. Turner, *The Police Establishment,* p. 52; Arthur Niederhoffer, *Behind the Shield: The Police in Urban Society* (Garden City, New York, 1969), p. 177; Herbert T. Klein, *The Police Damned if They Do—Damned if They Don't* (New York, 1968), pp. 209-210.

[48] Jerome H. Skolnick, *Justice Without Trial,* pp. 207-208.

[49] Richard Dougherty, "The New York Police," *Atlantic Monthly,* CCXXIX

HYPOTHESIS

A general hypothesis derived from the literature is that police officers engage in certain types of corrupt practices in accordance with a temporization process among four sets of uncomplimentary norms: (1) formal norms of the police organization, (2) informal norms of the police organization, (3) legal norms, (4) situational social meanings and rules, including trans-situational meanings from past socialization.

(February 1972). See also statement made by Knapp Commission concerning narcotics in New York City:

Narcotics: The Commission concurs with the statement by the State Commission of Investigation that Police officers in the Narcotics Division engage in "various types and techniques of corruption ranging from extortion, bribery, contradictory court testimony designed to affect the release of a narcotics criminal, improper associations with persons engaged in drug traffic, and finally . . . involvement by police officers in the actual sale of narcotics."
Commission to Investigate Alleged Police Corruption, *Interim Report on Investigative Phase,* p. 3.

Joseph McGovern, supervising assistant chief inspector commanding the New York City Internal Affairs Division, reports that "gambling graft is no longer the chief source of corruption—now it is narcotics." Fred J. Cook, "The Pusher-Cop: The Institutionalizing of Police Corruption," p. 26.

CHAPTER III

DIMENSIONS OF STUDY

INTRODUCTION

POLICE CORRUPTION occurs within a number of specific deviant (corrupt) patterns, each of which is analyzable along several dimensions: (1) acts and actors involved, (2) norm violations, (3) support from the peer group (fellow officers), (4) organizational degree of deviant practices, and (5) police department's reaction.

DIMENSIONS OF STUDY

ONE. There are at least two actors involved in most acts of police corruption, a corruptor and a corrupted police officer. The corruptor seeks some favor, preferential treatment or protection for his illicit or illegal activities. Corruptors may be absent from some patterns of police corruption e.g. police crimes against property such as burglary, but a corrupted officer is always present.

TWO. The acts may involve violations of formal departmental norms, legal norms, or a combination of these two.

THREE. The support and degree of support that acts of corruption receive from the police peer group will vary from act to act, with the identity of the corruptor and corrupted, informal peer group norms, and the situational context of the violations. For example, in a number of acts involving *clean* money the group may offer overt or covert approval. Actually, some types of corruption are seldom considered deviant, and in fact may be considered appropriate within certain situational contexts. In some departments anyone not engaging in these deviant acts would be labeled *deviant.*. Corrupt officers in these departments often openly brag about the amount of *clean* money they receive and ridicule uncorrupted officers. Frequently, acts involving *dirty* money are considered deviant by the peer group, and if engaged

[18]

in must be kept secret from other members of the police peer group.

The peer group is viewed as a microcoism of the organization, and it is assumed that sustained peer group support of certain corrupt acts reflects organizational support. The police peer group is defined as all working policemen within a specific police organization. Police departments have been defined by several scholars as *closed societies* jealous of their prerogatives, resentful of criticism and outside meddling, and anchored in tradition. Police departments function as *closed societies* because of the following characteristics: clannishness on and off duty; strong social identity within their occupational milieu, including a peculiar argot, conception of themselves as socially isolated; internal promotion from patrolman to supervisory positions which insures that all police personnel, at one time or another, experience similar occupational milieus; local recruitment from the same social stratum (lower-middle class); and familial and ethnic ties in many departments.[50] The closed and solidified nature of police personnel within a specific department tends to insure that police officers in that department share similar attitudes, feelings and definitions of situations. The assumed organizational support does not imply that all police organizations wholeheartedly approve of any or all corrupt police practices although most police administrators privately admit that the eradication of all types of corrupt police practices is impossible. *Police administrators are really concerned with how much and what types of corrupt police behavior should be permitted.*[51]

Four. Acts of corruption differ according to the degree of the organizational context in which they occur. Types representing adventitious corruption are not organized since they occur opportunistically. Other acts involving police protection of illegal activities are often highly organized.

Five. The kind and degree of the police department's reaction depends upon the type of corruption, the situational context of the

---

[50] For a discussion of the "closed society" concept see David J. Bordua and Albert J. Reiss, Jr., "Command, Control and Charisma: Reflections on Police Bureaucracy," *American Journal of Sociology,* 72:68-76 (July 1966); Jerome H. Skolnick, *Justice Without Trial,* pp. 42-62; Arthur Niederhoffer, *Behind the Shield;* William A. Westley, *Violence and the Police,* pp. 49-152; James Q. Wilson, *Varieties of Police Behavior,* pp. 27-30.

[51] Arthur Niederhoffer, *Behind the Shield,* p. 176; James Q. Wilson, *Varieties of Police Behavior,* pp. 109-112.

violation, the informal policy of the organization concerning *clean* and *dirty* money and public disclosure of the act and actor. Reactions fluctuate from indifference, acceptance, condonation, administrative ajudication, and disposition to criminal prosecution.

CHAPTER IV

TYPOLOGY OF POLICE CORRUPTION

INTRODUCTION

THIS CHAPTER postulates an empirical typology of police corruption which consists of eight unitary types: (1) Corruption of Authority, (2) Kickbacks, (3) Opportunistic Theft: from Arrestees, Victims, Crime Scenes and Unprotected Property, (4) Shakedowns, (5) Protection of Illegal Activities, (6) The Fix, (7) Direct Criminal Activities, and (8) Internal Pay-offs. Each of these types is analyzed by means of the five dimensions outlined in Chapter Three i.e. act and actors involved, norms violated, degree of peer group support, deviant organization and departmental reaction. The type nomenclature is based on modifications of definitions and terms on and about different forms of corrupt police behavior derived from these three sources: (1) critical content analysis of the literature, (2) patterns of police dishonesty discussed in Chapter Seven, "Police Integrity," Task Force Report: The Police,[52] and (3) observations by the senior author while employed as a police officer.

EIGHT TYPES OF POLICE CORRUPTION

Type One—Corruption of Authority

The officer's authority is corrupted when he receives officially unauthorized, unearned material gain by virtue of his position as a police officer without violating the law *per se*. Ostensibly, the officer receives free meals, liquor, commercial sex, free admissions to entertainment, police discounts on merchandise, services or other material inducements "just because the corruptor (supposedly) likes the police." In studies conducted in Boston, Chicago, and Washington, D. C.,

---

[52] The President's Commission on Law Enforcement and Administration of Justice, *Task Force Report: The Police,* pp. 208-212.

31 percent of all businessmen in wholesale or retail trade or business and repair services openly acknowledged favors to the police. Of those giving favors 43 percent gave free merchandise, food, or services to all policemen, and the remainder did so at discount. Presentation of self in uniform was all that was necessary to secure these benefits.[53] Additionally, rewards which violate departmental rules and regulations include payments by businessmen to police for property protection beyond routine duties, secret payments by property owners to police for arresting robbers and burglars at their establishments, *finders fee* payments by theft victims for recovery of their stolen property and payments by bondsmen bounty hunters to police for the arrest and notification of bond jumpers.[54] All of the above remunerations may be directly solicited, suggested, or unsolicited.[55] Professor Don L. Kooken, professor of police administration and a former police officer, believes "the public generally concedes that policemen are the world's greatest moochers," because of the prevalence of police acceptance of gifts, gratuities and rewards.[56]

The corruptors, for the most part, are respectable citizens "showing their gratitude for efficient police work." However, organized criminals also seize any opportunity to give a policeman something in hopes that "a lot of bread cast on the water will eventually be returned."[57] Acceptance of gifts, gratuities, and rewards from respectable merchants often marks the first step in the conditioning of an officer into other types of police corruption.[58] Even when the intentions of the cor-

---

[53] Albert J. Reiss, Jr., *The Police and the Public,* pp. 161-162.

[54] Rewards can (and do) have adverse consequences in police departments. They create jealousy among police officers, and they shift police interest away from areas which carry no reward to areas that do. Citizens Police Committee, *Chicago Police Problems* (Montclair, N. J., 1969; first published 1931), p. 58.

[55] In most instances, it is not necessary for officers to solicit these "fringe benefits," because the informal police network of communication obviates open solicitation—i.e. officers know which businesses offer them and which do not. Albert J. Reiss, Jr., *The Police and the Public,* p. 162.

[56] Quoted in Albert Deutsch, *The Trouble with Cops,* pp. 47-48.

[57] Ralph Salerno and John Tompkins, *The Crime Confederation,* p. 172.

[58] For a discussion of this conditioning process see Mort Stern, "What Makes a Policeman Go Wrong?" *Journal of Criminal Law, Criminology and Police Science,* 63: 98-101 (March 1962); William W. Turner, *The Police Establishment,* pp.51-52, Herbert T. Klein, *The Police, Damned if They Do—Damned if They Don't,* p. 193, William A. Westley, *Violence and the Police,* p. 72, James Q. Wilson, *Varieties of Police Behavior,* p. 207.

ruptor appear honorable, the officer's authority is corrupted because the acceptance of unauthorized goods or services obligates him to the corruptor. Most officers realize that businessmen and others make these supposedly gratuitous gestures for a reason; furthermore, most officers are aware that acceptance compromises their authority.[59]

Corrupt acts of this sort are usually defined as violations of departmental regulations but not as criminal violations. This behavior is corrupt because it violates the professed ethical norms of the policeman's office and departmental regulations. However, it is likely that most police peer groups support these gratuities (*goodies*) which they do not define as corrupt when received from noncriminals of high status.[60] Officers might rationalize these gifts as informal rewards deserved because of their low pay and hazardous working conditions; they are not breaking laws, merely receiving favors from grateful citizens. Often officers believe they are entitled to these informal remunerations because of the "divine right of police."[61] Some officers sanction businessmen and others who do not honor this "divine right," e.g. businesses are excluded from routine security checks; customers are harassed; citations are issued for obscure and seldom enforced violations; and property is sabotaged.

> This bum, the owner, I walk in here one cold day and he says, 'Have a cup of coffee, officer.' "I was froze blue so I took a cup. As I start to walk out he says, 'Ten cents, officer.' Loud he says it. Like he wants to embarrass me. "Oh, excuse me," I say. "I'm terribly sorry." I hand him the dime and then I go out. What do you think of a cheap bastard like that? So I decided to get even. Two can play the same game as one. I waited until I was in the drivers seat . . . That cheap bastard.[62]

---

[59] William A. Westley, *Violence and the Police*, p. 72.

[60] See St. Clari McKelway, "The Average Cop," in Gresham M. Sykes, and Thomas E. Drabeck (ed.) : *Law and the Lawless: A Reader in Criminology* (New York, 1969) pp. 392-395; Arthur Niederhoffer, *Behind the Shield,* p. 177; Albert J. Reiss, Jr., *The Police and the Public,* p. 162.

[61] David Burnham, "How Corruption is Built Into the System and a Few Ideas for What to Do About It," *New York,* Sept. 21, 1970, p. 30: "Police corruption begins with the notion that policemen by some peculiar divine right are entitled to free meals, free movies, and cut-rate prices on virtually everything they buy. This is known as "getting a break."

[62] This statement came from an officer who was discovered sticking toothpicks into the lock of a business establishment. Gene Radano, *Walking the Beat: A New York Policeman Tells What It's Like on His Side of the Law* (Cleveland, 1968), pp. 140-141.

Hear what Kennedy did yesterday? He goes in for a cup of coffee and as he's about to walk out the Greek says, 'Ten cents.' Kennedy goes through the act. 'Oh, excuse me,' he says. He looks at his watch and says, 'I might as well have another cup of coffee, I still got time.' The Greek starts to refill Kennedy's cup when our boy in blue says. 'Oh I'm terribly sorry, sir. But pouring coffee in a dirty cup: that's a violation of the sanitary code.' And he writes him out a summons.

That's sticking it up a guy's moon and breaking it off.[63]

In departments where the acceptance of gratuities is a routinzed custom, the officer who refuses to accept them is frequently considered a deviant by his peer group.

Many police departments, though public disavowing this behavior, accept it as a system of informal rewards, particularly if the officers receiving the gratuities are otherwise acceptable to the department and if the corruptors are respectable citizens and adept at smoothly and surreptitiously rendering the rewards.[64] Informal organizational policy usually condones these unorganized practices, and reaction is likely to vary from acceptance to mild disapproval.

Type Two—Kickbacks

In many communities police officers receive goods services, or money for referring business to towing companies, ambulances, garages, lawyers, doctors, bondsmen, undertakers, taxi-cabs, service stations, moving companies and others who are anxious to sell services or goods to persons with whom the police interact during their routine patrol.[65] Corruptors are usually legitimate businessmen and profes-

---

[63] *Ibid.,* pp. 29-30.

[64] For a discussion of organizations allowing forbidden activities to function as a system of informal rewards see Jack D. Douglas, *American Social Order* (New York, 1971), pp. 163-166. See also Albert J. Reiss, Jr., *The Police and the Public,* pp. 161-163.

[65] For a general discussion of kickback arrangements between police and businessmen see The President's Commission on Law Enforcement and Administration of of Justice, *Task Force Report: The Police,* pp. 208-209. Deutsch reports of police being paid for delivering dead bodies to undertaker parlors. The standard kickback was ten dollars per body. Albert Deutsch, *The Trouble with Cops,* p. 46. In 1963, thirty Illinois state troopers were suspended for accepting kickbacks from tow-truck drivers. Two of the drivers had carried on such arrangements with the police for over ten years. Ralph L. Smith, *The Tarnished Badge,* pp. 149-150. For a more recent account of police collusions with two-truck drivers see Com-

sionals who stand to gain through a *good* working relationship with the police. Within some departments, officers seek and hotly vie for certain work assignments because of the availability of kickbacks in these details e.g. traffic accident investigation, especially those units that investigate serious injuries and fatalities which almost always result in civil litigation (lawyer-police conspiracy), complaint desk assignments (lawyers, bondsman-police conspiracy), bond details (bondsmen-police conspiracy).[66] Kickbacks violate departmental norms but are not generally defined or acted upon as criminal violations.

The peer group may support kickbacks from legitimate businessmen as *clean* fringe benefits earned by virtue of their position. Many officers who refuse all kickbacks are labelel deviant by some peer groups. The degree of peer group support depends on the following contingencies: trustworthiness, reputation, status, and affluence of the corruptor, adeptness of the corruptor in presenting his rewards as *clean* money, and the secrecy of the situation.

Kickback organization inheres in the collusion between businessmen and policemen. Businessmen frequently distribute cards to police officers indicating their willingness to transact business. Some arrangements, formal or otherwise, must operate in the determination of payments to the policemen who make the referrals i.e. certain amounts of goods, services, or money for specified referrals.

Many departments condone or overlook kickbacks so long as the corruptor is a legitimate businessman or professional, the corrupted officer is otherwise acceptable to the department and the value of the goods and services is held to a minimum. However, many departments will react negatively to kickbacks in cash. Department's condonation of kickbacks is based on the following situational contingencies: informal definition of *clean* money, discretionary and secrecy

---

mission to Investigate Alleged Police Corruption, *Interim Report on Investigative Phase,* p. 5.

[66] In the department Westley studied, desk sergeants informed bondsmen and attorneys whenever a prisoner needed their services. The bondsmen and attorneys gave the desk man a percentage of the fees they collected. At one time the chief in this department issued a listing of approved bondsmen and attorneys who paid the chief a set percentage. The chief, in turn, paid the desk sergeant and sometimes the arresting officers received a regular monthly stipend. William A. Westley, *Violence and the Police,* p. 33.

measures utilized by corruptors and corrupted, the status and reputation of the corruptor. In communities where such working arrangements are traditional among policemen, businessmen and professionals, the police establishment may offend the legitimate business and professional community by strong overt reaction. Departmental reaction varies from acceptance to mild sanctions in the case of goods and services; however, cash kickbacks may result in stronger disciplinary action i.e. suspension or dismissal.

Type Three—Opportunistic Theft: From Arrestees, Victims, Crime Scenes and Unprotected Property

These acts do not involve any corruptor, only the corrupt officer and unsuspecting victims. Rolled arrestees, traffic accident victims and unconscious or dead citizens are unaware of the act.[67] Officers investigating burglaries may take merchandise or money left behind by the orginal thief.[68] Officers may also take items from unprotected property sites discovered during routine security patrol e.g. merchandise or money from unlocked businesses, building supplies from construction locations, unguarded items from business or industrial establishments.[69] Finally, policemen may keep a portion of the confiscated

---

[67] Messick gives an account of a Miami police officer who made a career of stealing valuables from dead bodies and receiving stolen property. This same officer was allowed to quietly resign without indictment and subsequently was employed as a policeman by another police organization. Hank Messick, *Syndicate in the Sun,* p. 151.

[68] In a study conducted by Reiss, participant observers in two cities observed officers taking merchandise from burglarized businesses. Albert J. Reiss, Jr., *The Police and the Public,* p. 158. Some officers rationalize their thefts by the reflection that nobody will suffer because "it's insured." One Los Angeles policeman put it this way:

> It's three in the morning and you're on patrol and you hear a burglar alarm. You find the back door of a jewelry store open and inside the place is turned upside down. Someone has taken a lot of stuff, but he had to leave in a hurry and there's a lot more lying around. There's nobody within six blocks to see what you're doing. You know the stuff's insured anyway. So what do you do?

Fred J. Cook, The Corrupted Land: *The Social Morality of Modern America,* (New York, 1966), p. 244.

[69] For a general discussion of opportunistic theft, and a specific commentary on "toting" (thefts from unprotected property) see The President's Commission on

evidence they discover during vice raids e.g. money, liquor, narcotics and property.[70] All of these behaviors violate departmental and criminal norms.

Peer group support rests on the peer group's informal policy of accepting or rejecting *clean* money, the definition of *clean* money (the smaller the amount of money and the smaller the worth of the article taken, the cleaner the money) and *dirty* money, and the umbrella of secrecy within the situation.

Most police departments react negatively to this opportunistic and unorganized type of theft. Reaction is usually contingent upon (1) the department's informal definition of *clean* money, (2) the value of the theft, (3) the public disclosure of the corrupt officer, and (4) willingness of the victim to prosecute. Sanctions vary from mild disapproval, admonitions and warnings to suspensions, dismissals and criminal proceedings.

Type Four—Shakedowns

Shakedowns arise opportunistically i.e. the officer inadvertently witnesses or gains knowledge of a criminal violation and violator and subsequently accepts a bribe for not making an arrest. The corruptor may be a *respectable* citizen who offers a bribe to an officer to avoid a traffic charge[71] or a criminal adventitiously caught in the commission of an illegal act who induces the officer to free him. Many professional criminals carry what is known in the criminal argot as *fall money*, a sum of money carried on their person that can be used to bribe an officer should they be appreheneded while committing a crime.[72] Shakedowns are engaged in with relative impunity because

---

Law Enforcement and Administration of Justice, *Task Force Report: The Police*, p. 210.

[70] In 1971, one New York City police precinct was unable to account for 68.25 pounds of heroin (worth roughly seven million dollars). Richard Dougherty, "The New York Police," *Atlantic Monthly*, 224: 6, (February 1972).

[71] In Chicago during the early 1960's, it was a universal practice for citizens to keep a five dollar bill clipped to their drivers license. When stopped for a traffic violation the driver would hand the license to the policeman who would remove the five dollars and wave the driver on. Ralph L. Smith, *The Tarnished Badge*, pp. 176-177. Recently, this practice is reported to occur in New York City, except the amount of money offered has risen to ten dollars. David Burnham, "How Corruption is Built into the System," p. 30.

[72] Congressman Charles B. Rangel, 18th Congressional District New York City,

the victim is unlikely to complain since he is engaged in some form of illegal activity. The cardinal rule among officers who engage in shakedowns is "don't come back" i.e. make arrangements to meet the victim at a later time, in order to give the victim an opportunity to contact other law enforcement officers and set a trap. Shakedowns violate both departmental and criminal norms; they are punishable under bribery statutes. The corruptor and the officer are equally guilty of a crime.

Officers who take bribes from transporters of contraband such as gambling paraphernalia, bootleg liquor, or money from traffic violators are not considered deviant among peer groups who make distinctions between *clean* and *dirty* money. Even officers who do not engage in any forms of corruption are likely to maintain a code of silence when learning of these acts. On the other hand, taking bribes from certain kinds of felons e.g. narcotics pushers, burglars, or robbers who offer *dirty* money, is considered deviant by most police peer groups. The situational contingencies that determine the susceptible officer's actions related to shakedowns are the trustworthiness, reputation, status, and affluence of the victim, the victim's front and presentation of self,[73] the umbrella of secrecy that covers the negotiating circumstances.

Departmental reactions to shakedowns, unorganized criminal acts, fluctuate with the definition of and the informal policy toward *clean* and *dirty* money. Most departments, even those open to other types of corruption, react negatively to shakedowns because they quickly give the department a bad reputation. Departments that tacitly condone shakedowns are concerned with the selectivity of the victim e.g. transporters of contraband, out-of-town drivers, and low class,

---

states "that before a narcotics pusher begins selling narcotics in Harlem he must have $1,000 cash on him, and this is to make certain that, even if he is picked up, he will never make it to court because this cash allows him to buy his way out of it." Fred J. Cook, "The Pusher Cop," p. 24.

Bookies and other professional gamblers also carry *fall money*. One bookie stated that most of his payoffs to the police had been for "getting out of" arrests. It was his practice to meet his employees at night on a supermarket lot to exchange cash and betting slips; therefore, he always carried extra cash to bribe police who discovered this exchange. Michael J. Hindelang, "Bookies and Bookmaking: A Descriptive Analysis, *Crime and Delinquency,* 17: 253 (July 1971).

[73] Erving Goffman, *The Presentation of Self in Everyday Life* (New York, 1959).

powerless citizens are often considered fair game.[74] Publicly exposed officers are usually heavily sanctioned e.g. dismissal and/or criminal prosecution.

Type Five—Protection of Illegal Activities

In this type corruptors are actively engaged in illegal activities and seek to operate without police harassment by offering some reward to members of the police organization. So-called victimless crimes (frequently in violation of unenforceable laws) including vice operations pertaining to gambling, illegal drug sales, prostitution, liquor violations, abortion rings, pornography rings, homosexual establishments, after hours clubs, frequently designate police protected enterprises.[75] Officers in some departments also receive protection payoffs from robbers, burglars, jewel thieves, confidence men, fences and forgers.[76] Legitimate businesses operating illegally often pay for protection e.g. some cab companies and individual cab drivers pay police officers for the illegal permission to operate outside prescribed routes and areas, to pick up and discharge fares at unauthorized sites, to operate cabs that do not meet safety and cleanliness standards, or to operate without proper licensing procedures. Trucking firms pay for the privilege of hauling overloaded cargoes and driving off

---

[74] In the police department Westley studied, the traffic division was considered a desirable detail because of the easy access to shakedowns. Out-of-town drivers were logical victims because they were susceptible to a large fine and bond, also they were unlikely to have connections in town. William A. Westley, *Violence and the Police,* pp. 33-34.

[75] For a discussion of police corruption and vice operations see Edwin M. Schur, *Crimes Without Victims—Deviant Behavior and Public Policy: Abortion, Homosexuality, Drug Addiction* (Englewood Cliffs, 1965). One researcher has attributed the high cost of abortions to police corruption. "Payoffs to police officers are accepted by all abortionists as a necessary annoyance and this expense is passed on to the patient." Lucy Freeman, *The Abortionists* (New York, 1962), p. 202, quoted in Edwin M. Schur, *Crimes Without Victims,* p. 34.

[76] Excerpt from Dade County Florida Grand Jury Report (1968):

There was evidence of burglaries, thefts and similar crimes being planned and carried into effect with the knowledge of deputies. There was testimony that burglars and thiefs were required to report the amount of their hauls and to divide with officers of the law.

Hank Messick, *Syndicate in the Sun,* p. 228.

prescribed truck routes.[77] Legitimate businesses may pay police officers
to avoid Sunday *blue* laws.[78] Construction companies in some cities
pay police officers to overlook violations of city regulations e.g. trucks
blocking traffic, violating pollution guidelines (burning trash, creating
dust), destroying city property, and blocking sidewalks.[79] Regular
operation of all the above enterprises indicates police collusion with
illegal operators, and most of these operations function within criminal organizations. These regular operations are open in the sense
that several groups and segments of the population are familiar with
them, although the attendant conspiracy arrangements generally remain secret.[80] These police collusions and conspiracies with illegal
enterprises break both formal departmental and criminal norms.

---

[77] In 1962, an investigation uncovered that Illinois state troopers were accepting
pay-offs from 90 trucking firms operating in and out of Chicago. The firms were
allowed to operate with overloaded trucks. Payoffs ranged from seventy-five dollars for captains to ten dollars for troopers. The pay-offs were mailed to the
trooper's homes with the firms business card attached. Ralph L. Smith, *The
Tarnished Badge,* pp. 148-149.

[78] David Burnham, "Graft Here Said to Run Into Millions," *New York Times,*
119: 18 (April 25, 1970).

[79] Commission to Investigate Alleged Police Corruption, *Interim Report on Investigative Phase,* p. 5.

[80] In June, 1971, four United States Senators—Harold Hughes (D., Iowa),
Chairman of the Senate Committee on Alcoholism and Narcotics; Jacob A. Javits
(R., N.Y.), Harrison A. Williams (D., N.J.) and Richard S. Schweiker (R., Pa.)
made a visit to a methadone treatment clinic in Harlem Hospital. The director
of the hospital gave ten dollars to a young boy, and the senators watched as the
boy went across the street and purchased five glassine bags of heroin. The senators were then taken to a shooting gallery (argot: place where addicts meet to
inject narcotics) and observed addicts injecting heroin. Senator Hughes made
the following statement:

> When it's so open that U.S. Senators can walk just across the street
> from a hospital where addicts are supposed to be recovering, when heroin
> can be bought on any street, then its a national tragedy.

Fred J. Cook, "The Pusher Cop," pp. 28-30. See also Judge George Edwards,
The Police on the Urban Frontier: A Guide to Community Understanding (New
York, 1968), pp. 31-32:

> In poor areas, especially Negro ghettos, organized crime operates on a
> scale that is widely known. The residents seeing these operate openingly
> assume that the police are in league with the operators. They know that
> whenever a numbers house, a walk-in bookie, an unlicensed drinking
> place or a house of prostitution operates there must be corruption.

Peer group support is dependent on the peer group's policy of accepting or rejecting *clean* money, the informal definition of *clean* and *dirty* money, the trustworthiness, status (position, respectability, influence, prestige, authority, and power in the underworld and/or upperworld) and affluence of the corruptor, and the situational facility of secret and secure transactions.[81] Police who receive protection money as well as many community members view some forms of this type of corruption as a necessary, regulated, patterned evasion i.e. a publicly accepted norm is covertly violated on a large scale with the tacit acceptance or approval of the same society or group, at least as long as such corruption is concealed.[82] Although the community may desire the illegal services and goods regulated by protection money, officers (even those not on the take) who fail to enforce the law in this area are compromised and corrupted by their inaction.[83] Contrariwise, those officers who attempt to enforce unsupported laws which sanction *protected* goods and services may be thwarted e.g. arrestees are freed because of insufficient evidence, small fines and/or sentences are dispensed, judges and prosecuting attorneys chastise and discourage officers for *overzealousness* in this area, cases are quashed or *nolle prossed.*[84] *This dilemma functions to drive many honest and dedicated officers to resignation, ritualism, inaction, or corruption. Moreover, community approval of "protected" illegal goods and services militates for a thoroughly deviant and criminal police organization.* Often what the community fails to recognize is that "a cop bought by gamblers can also be bought by burglars.[85]

A high degree of organization is usually present in this type. For

---

[81] See Jerome H. Skolnick, *Justice Without Trial*, pp. 207-208.

[82] Albert J. Reiss, Jr., "The Study of Deviant Behavior," p. 58; Howard E. Freeman and Wyatt C. Jones, *Social Problems: Causes and Controls* (Chicago, 1970), p. 235.

[83] Donald R. Cressey, *Theft on the Nation* (New York, 1969), p. 289:

Even if the violation is overlooked diplomatically, in the interests of community peace and harmony . . . He (police officer) is "in" and he must play the game.

[84] For a discussion of these practices see Ralph L. Smith, *The Tarnished Badge,* pp. 76-77; John A. Gardiner, *The Politics of Corruption,* p. 66; William A. Westley, *Violence and the Police,* p. 143; James Q. Wilson, *Varieties of Police Behavior,* p. 105.

[85] Hand Messick, *Syndicate in the Sun,* pp. 8-9.

protection to be successful, several members of the police organization must know what places, businesses and persons enjoy immunity;
systems of ongoing communication must be insured; pay-offs and
kinds of police protection must be negotiated i.e with the criminal
organization.   Because of increased specalization brought about by
attempts to professionalize police departments, it is not necessary to
pay-off all members of a police organization.   Only the detail which
handles the relevant activity—cab detail, safe burglary, forgery, vice-
squad—must be corrupted.   The classic technique employed by
organized crime is known as the *vice-squad pattern*.   Police action
against organized crime is usually centralized in the vice-squad.   Any
officer who receives information concerning organized crime delivers
this knowledge to members of the vice-squad.   Therefore, organized
criminals only need to corrupt this detail to insure protection.   This
pattern partly originated for economical reasons; it cuts down on
operating expenses.[86]

Protection of illegal vice operators may be so complete in some
departments that officers who inadvertantly arrest *protected* operators
must pay a fine to the corrupt officers who have illegally licensed the
vice operators.[87]   Protection money also requires illegal routinized
departmental procedures and sanctions against uncooperating operators.   Sanctions vary from harassment and arrest to murder.[88]   There
is usually a distribution of pay-offs with all members of vice details

---

[86] For a discussion of this "vice-squad pattern" see, Donald R. Cressey, *Theft
of the Nation,* p. 264.

[87] See *Ibid.,* pp. 261-262. For illegal licensing and police fining one another see,
David Burnham, "Gamblers Links to Police Lead to Virtual Licensing," *New
York Times,* 119: 1 (April 26, 1970).

... if a plain clothesman arrests a gambler who is on the *pad* by mis-
take he also will be fined—maybe a hundred bucks or so.

The *pad* is a list of establishments—either legal or illegal—which provides
policemen with regular payments, usually on a monthly basis. There is also a
"Christmas Pad." See "Police Use Own Words to Speak of Corruption," *New
York Times,* 119: 18 (April 25, 1970).

[88] Violence, including murder, has been used by some police officers when
operators of illegal enterprises have refused to pay bribes. In 1912, a New York
City police lieutenant was convicted and sent to the electric chair for the murder
of a racketeer who refused to pay off. William W. Turner, *The Police Establishment,* p. 49. For a more recent account of the connection between violence and
pay-offs see allegations that Chicago police officers murdered heroin wholesalers
who refused or stopped pay-offs to members of the police department. "Chicago

receiving prorated shares of the action. Officers transferred from lucrative vice details to less desirable (in this case, less profitable assignments) often continue to draw for a specified time their former share of the protection money as "severance pay."[89] Protection money organization may resemble an interlocking bureaucracy as a sub-organization representing the police and organized crime. The degree and extent of organization may (and often does) penetrate and include other municipal governmental institutions.[90]

Departmental reaction hinges on the degree of its involvement with criminal organizations or legitimate businesses that operate illegally, informal definition of *clean* money, identity of the corruptor, and whether or not there is public disclosure of flagrant violations. If department involvement is deep and widespread, exposed and publicly identified officers will usually be allowed to resign as quietly as possible in order to prevent any large scale investigations. On the other hand, should strong pressure for sanctions be exerted by legal systems and community organizations without the police establishment (e.g. local district attorneys, investigating commissions, county and state police agencies, chamber of commerces, news media), the disclosed officers would probably be dismissed and criminally charged. Sanctioned officers (even those convicted of criminal violations) usually accept their fate as an illegal occupational hazard. Furthermore, those who wish to testify and implicate others are rarely able to supply sufficient evidence to invoke indictments of their peers or supervisors who are also receiving protection money.

Police departments with informal policies that condone the accep-

---

Cops Under Fire," *Time,* July 10, 1972, p. 22.

[89] Richard Dougherty, "The New York Police," p. 6:

If an unlucky fellow happened to be transferred to another command—where there was often a wait before he could get on the pad there—he would often continue to draw his old share for two months.

See also "Cops on the Take," *Newsweek,* Nov. 1, 1971, p. 48.

. . . And when an officer was transferred out of plain clothes into a less lucrative pose, he was awarded an extra two months worth of the pad as severance pay. "Is that to tide you over before you can get on the next one?" asked Knapp Commissioner Joseph Monserrat. "It gets you back on your feet, yes sir," replied Phillips.

[90] John A. Gardiner, *The Politics of Corruption.*

tance of protection money attempt to block investigations by any persons, groups or organizations, at times with the aid of criminals or other corrupt legal systems (e.g. corrupt district attorneys, mayors, political bosses, city, county and state officials) within the administration of justice.[91]   Aid in this direction may take the form of physical violence against person or property or *devious* legal and/or administrative procedures within or without the police organization.

Type Six—The Fix

Two sub-types constitute the fix: (1) the quashing of prosecution proceedings following the offender's arrest and (2) the *taking up* (disposal of record) of traffic tickets.   Corruptors are arrestees attempting to avoid court action and citizens seeking to avoid blemished driving records.   The fixer in criminal cases is often a detective or some other designated police officer who conducts or controls the investigation upon which the prosecution proceedings are based.[92] Prior to or at the preliminary hearing is the optimum period to fix a criminal case; should the case proceed to the grand jury or trial court stage, it becomes more difficult and more expensive to effect a fix.[93]   Therefore, investigating police officers are in the most advantageous position to effect the fix, though district attorneys and judges may be involved in the criminal fix at later stages.   The investigating officer usually agrees to "sell the case," that is, "withdraw prosecution," in return for some material reward; he either fails to request prosecution, tampers with the existing evidence, or gives perjured testimony.   The case may be sold directly to the criminal by the investigating officer or negotiated by a go-between e.g. jailer, lawyer, police officer, bail bondsman.   Chambliss reports the case of a professional safecracker who was able to avoid prosecution in all but five of three hundred arrests spanning a forty-year period.[94]   In some

---

[91] See Hank Messick, *Syndicate in the Sun.*

[92] For an historical account of the fix see Edwin H. Sutherland, "The Fix," in William J. Chambliss (ed.): Crime and the Legal Process (New York, 1969) pp. 261-264.

[93] Gresham M. Sykes, *Crime and Society* 2nd ed. (New York, 1967), p. 151.

[94] William J. Chambliss, *Crime and the Legal Process,* p. 93. In the department Westley studied the fix was prevalent in the police court which handled misdemeanor cases. The same activity took place in the county criminal court, but to a lesser degree and with more secrecy. William A. Westley, *Violence and the Police,* pp. 37-38.

police departments it is even possible to fix homicide cases and felonious aggravated assaults against police officers.[95]

The traffic fixer is usually the ticketing officer who subsequently agrees to dispose of the ticket for a fee. Other police officers who have control of the traffic ticketing process at any time after the original citation may also fix tickets e.g. supervisory officers or desk sergeants who have access to ticket records. Contact with the fixer may be made directly by the citizen or by a designated go-between e.g. another police officer. The fix (both sub-types) violate departmental and criminal norms.

Peer groups overtly oppose the sale of felony cases; however, a conspiracy of silence in some police departments lends covert support to individual officers who might engage in this activity. The selling of misdemeanor cases and the fixing of traffic tickets is not as seriously frowned upon in those peer groups that accept *clean* money.

Departmental reaction to the fixing of criminal cases is generally severe i.e. dismissal and/or criminal prosecution. Even police departments that condone the fix are likely to sanction publicly exposed police officers. Reaction will vary with the status, reputation, and affluence of the corruptor, the department's informal policy concerning *clean* money, and the secrecy of the transaction. Reaction will range from acceptance to administrative suspension or dismissal.

Type Seven—Direct Criminal Activities

This type involves no corruptor. Policemen directly commit crimes against the person or property of another for material gain, acts

---

[95] Tom Buckley, "Murphy Among the Meat Eaters," *New York Times Magazine,* 119: 44 (Dec. 19, 1971).

Supervising Chief Inspector Syndney Cooper answered: "There are three kinds of men in the department . . . I call them the birds, the grass eaters and the meat eaters. The birds just fly up high. They don't eat anything either because they are honest or because they don't have any good opportunities. You've got to figure that half of the force is in jobs—the Tactical Patrol Force and the Safety Division, for example—where there are little or no pick-ups. The grass-eaters, well they'll accept a cup of coffee or a free meal or a television set wholesale from a merchant, but they draw a line. The meat-eaters are different. They're out looking. They're on a pad with gamblers, they deal in junk, or they'd compromise a homicide investigation for money. . . ."

which are clear violation of both departmental and criminal norms. These actions receive little support from most police peer groups (usually not even from peer groups engaged in other types of corruption). Direct criminal activities, burglary and robbery, are defined as extreme forms of *dirty* money crimes, and those who do engage in them do so at great peril—even from most of their colleagues on the force.[96] Generally, some organization is connected with this type. Groups of police officers operate (as burglars and robbers) in small working groups similar to the modus operandi of professional criminals.[97]

Departmental reaction is generally severe. Departments that tolerate other forms of corruption will usually prosecute and send to prison officers discovered engaging in forms of direct criminal activities.

Type Eight—Internal Pay-Offs

Internal pay-offs regulate a market where police officer's prerogative may be bought, bartered or sold. Actors in this type, both corcuptors and corrupted, are exclusively police officers. Prerogatives negotiated encompass work assignments, off-days, holidays, vacation periods, control of evidence and promotions. Officers who administer the distribution of assignments and personnel may collect fees for

---

[96] Since 1960 a number of police burglary rings have been uncovered in a variety of police departments—e.g. Denver, Colo.; Chicago, Ill.; Nassau County, New York; Des Moines, Iowa; Nashville and Memphis, Tenn.; Birmingham, Ala.; Cleveland, Ohio; Bristol, Conn.; Burlington, Vermont; and Miami, Fla. See Ralph L. Smith, *The Tarnished Badge;* Hank Messick, *Syndicate in the Sun;* James Q. Wilson, *Varieties of Police Behavior;* Fred J. Cook, *The Corrupted Land.*

Fred J. Cook, *The Corrupted Land,* p. 243.

Burglars in blue have turned up in police force after police force in such numbers that they cannot be dismissed with the comfortable rationalization that "there are always a few bad apples in the barrel." These burglars in uniform have been organized into such bands that they have constituted 8 to 10 percent of a city's entire constabulary.

[97] The Denver police burglars in the early 1960's were professional safecrackers. They were so proficient at safecracking that one *safe job* was completed in seventeen minutes start to finish. The three principal members of the group were probably the most experienced safecrackers in the nation at that time; they were able to *crack* a supposedly burglar proof safe, a Diebold 10 with three inch thick steel walls. Ralph L. Smith, *The Tarnished Badge,* pp. 14-31.

assigning officers to certain divisions, precincts, units, details, shifts, and beats and for insuring that certain personnel are retained in, tranferred from or excluded from certain work assignments.[98] In some departments where members receive protection money from vice operations, officers contact command personnel and bid for *good* (lucrative) assignments. Usually, everything else being equal, the profitable assignments go to the highest bidder. Certain off-days and selected vacation periods are sometimes sold by supervisory personnel e.g. an officer who wishes to be off on the weekend, who wishes to avoid split off-days, or who desires a vacation during peak summer months may pay his supervisor for these privileges. Members of a police department whose prerogatives include the control of criminal evidence (e.g. investigating officers, detectives, evidence technicians, desk sergeants) may well sell this evidence e.g. wire taps, fingerprints, forged documents, contraband, and other physical evidence or instrumentalities of the crime) to an officer who in turn uses it in a shakedown or fix.[99]

Most peer groups probably do not support this blatant and criminal activity which results in their own exploitation and victimization. On the other hand, peer groups engaged in other types of illegal corruption, protection money, shakedowns, and fixes, might accept internal pay-offs as necessary and inevitable. Officers in certain assignments have little opportunity to engage in other types of corrupt activities. Internal pay-offs provide these officers with an illegitimate opportunity structure.[100]

---

[98] David Burnham, "Graft Here Said to Run Into Millions," p. 18:

I was recently a patrolman, a sergeant said. In my precinct you were supposed to pay for getting a good post. It's so systematized that the roll-call man actually would know in a dollar figure how many pickups were on your post and you were supposed to kick in accordingly.

[99] "Cops on the Take," *Newsweek,* p. 48:

Phillips told the committee how . . . detectives regularly bought and sold wiretap evidence on gambling houses for use in "scoring" the operation for extra cash. ("Scoring" is the New York police argot for shakedowns.) Some officers break departmental regulations by retaining physical evidence in their possession until prosecution proceedings to prevent their sale or destruction within a corrupt department.

[100] David Burnham, "Graft Here Said To Run Into Millions," p. 18:

Internal pay-offs are often highly organized within departments engaged in illegal types of corruption. Departmental reaction varies with the department's involvement in other types of illegal corruption, the secrecy of the arrangement, and the willingness of the officers involved to expose and prosecute fellow officers. Reaction varies from acceptance and protection to exposure and dismissal or criminal prosecution.

SUMMARY

The postulated typology does not infer a universality of any one or more types of police corruption divorced from cultural, temporal, or spatial dimensions. Norms, rules and sanctioning procedures pertaining to police corrupt behavior are relative in time and space and therefore the typology would have to be empirically tested, retested and modified accordingly. Various types of police corruption may be ushered in and out of any one police organization over time periods —corrupt styles come and go. Some types may be created within the context of the local situation or diffused from without.

The eight types of police corrupt behavior are arranged in a hierarchal fashion from rule breaking to lawless behavior. (see Table 1.) This arrangement suggests a progressive process in dynamics, accretion, and gravity, a process that might be checked or altered at any one or more levels of progression by the tolerance limits of the police organization or the community. In police organizations where several types of corrupt behavior exist, the police department operates in a systematically lawless manner.[101]

Corruption of authority, type one, could probably endure for long periods without effecting serious breaches in the legitimate duties and functions of a police organization; however, this type of behavior

---

The men assigned to enforcing the gambling laws, for example, are expected to give the precinct desk officer a $5 tip for each gambler that the plainclothes man arrests and the desk officer must process. Of course a gambling arrest is a lot of work for the desk officer, a senior officer explained. But the real reason for the tip is that the desk officer knows the plainclothes man is making a lot of money—that the arrest usually is in some way phoney—and he wants a share of the pie.

[101] For a discussion of police departments operating in a systematically lawless manner see Edwin H. Sutherland, *Principles of Criminology* 4th ed. (Chicago, 1947), pp. 236-237.

marks the first step in the temporization process leading to other types of corrupt behavior. Officers who accept gratuities are more likely to accept kickbacks, type two, than officers who decline gratuities.

Small thefts from crime scenes, type three, may be rationalized by some officers in departments where corruption of authority and kickbacks are unsanctioned. The police peer group's distinction between *clean* and *dirty* money thefts will usually lead to serious thefts. When some members of a police department engage in serious thefts and other members do not report this behavior, the organization has begun to operate in a lawless manner.

Shakedowns, type four, are engaged in by the more deviant members of the lawless peer group. At this juncture many uncompromised officers become disillusioned with police work and resign. When uncorrupted officers leave the police organization or remain and become implicated in corruption by their adherence to the *code of silence,* the stage is set for type five, protection of illegal activities. Although this type has received the most extensive treatment in the literature (most writers consider no other type of police corruption), *illegal operators and legitimate companies operating illegally would probably find it hard to corrupt members of a police organization who do not engage in other types of corruption.* When members of a police organization accept protection money with impunity, the police organization in which they work begins to shift its function from law enforcement to the unlawful regulation of criminal activities.

The fix, type six, operates in all departments that accept protection money. Police organizations that condone the acceptance of protection money and the fix eventually leave themselves open to type seven, direct criminal activities. Police officers without a work detail that insures them an adequate share of the available graft may decide to cure their relative deprivation through and by direct criminal activities. Some may draw no fine distinction between money derived from robberies and burglaries and scarce *clean* money.

Internal pay-offs, type eight, mark the last step in the progression to a thoroughly deviant and criminal police organization. There is a great likelihood that all of the preceeding types of police corruption will inhere in the police organization characterized by a routinized system of internal pay-offs. Internal pay-offs provide an ultimate illegal opportunity structure for all members of the police organization.

Table 1. TYPOLOGY OF POLICE CORRUPTION

Dimensions of Study	1 Corruption of Authority	2 Kickbacks
Act and Actors Involved	*Acts* Free meals, liquor, services, discounts, free admissions to entertainment and rewards	*Acts* Money, goods and services from towing companies, ambulances, garages, lawyers, doctors, bondsmen, undertakers, taxicabs, service stations, moving companies, etc.
	Corruptors Respectable citizens	*Corruptors* Legitimate business
Norms Violated	Violation of departmental regulations Not usually defined as criminal	Violation of departmental norms Not generally defined or acted upon as criminal violations
Support from Peer Group	High Many groups consider this non-deviant behavior when coming from noncriminals of high status	High Viewed as "clean" fringe benefits
Organization Content	Low No organization	High Collusion between businessmen and policemen
Police Department's Reaction	Low Acceptance or mild disapproval	Medium Acceptance and mild disapproval for goods and services, suspension or dismissal for cash kickbacks.

TYPOLOGY OF POLICE CORRUPTION—continued

3	4
Opportunistic Theft: From Arrestees, Victims, Crime Scenes and Unprotected Property	Shakedowns

Acts	*Acts*
Thefts from arrestees, victims, crime scenes and unprotected property	Money from criminal or traffic violators

Corruptors	*Corruptors*
Corrupt officers and unsuspecting victims	Criminals or citizens
Violation of criminal norms	Violation of criminal norms
Larceny, grand and petty	Extortion

Medium	Low
Depends on: peer groups, informal policy of accepting or rejecting "clean" money, value of the theft and the secrecy of the theft	Degree of support contingent on: informal policy concerning "clean" money, identity of corruptor and secrecy of the act

Low	Low
No organization—opportunistic	No organization—opportunistic

Medium	Medium
Mild disapproval, admonitions and warnings, suspensions, dismissals, and criminal proceedings	Suspension or dismissal

TYPOLOGY OF POLICE CORRUPTION—continued

5 Protection of Illegal Activities	6 The Fix
Acts	*Acts*
Protection money from vice operators or legitimate companies operating illegally	(1) Quashing of prosecution proceedings
	(2) Disposal of traffic tickets
Corruptors	*Corruptors*
Criminals and legitimate businessmen	Criminals and citizens
Violation of criminal norms	Violation of criminal norms
Bribery	Bribery
Medium	Medium
Hinges on policy of accepting or rejecting "clean" money, identity of the corruptor and the secrecy of the transaction	Most peer groups oppose sale of criminal cases, although some may condone sale of misdemeanor cases and fixing traffic tickets
High	Midium
Exhibits bureaucratic structure	Fixers may be maintained on a payroll
Low	High
Departments may block investigations	Dismissal and/or criminal prosecution

7 Direct Criminal Activities	8 Internal Payoffs
Acts	*Acts*
Burglaries, robberies	Sale of work assignments, off-days, holidays, vacation periods, evidence and promotion
No Corruptors	*Corruptors*
Policemen directly commit crimes against persons or property	Exclusively police officers
Violation of criminal norms	Violation of criminal norms
Burglary and robbery	Extortion and bribery
Low	Low
No support from peer group	Most peer groups oppose this criminal activity
Low	Low
Small working groups of corrupt officers	May be organized within departments engaged in illegal types of corruption
High	Medium
Dismissal and criminal prosecution	Varies from acceptance and protection to dismissal or criminal prosecution

CHAPTER V

IMPLEMENTATION OF TYPOLOGY

INTRODUCTION

AN EMPIRICAL typology's principal function is to chart the actual behavior patterns displayed by specific kinds of individuals. The typology should reflect precisely and completely patterns that exist in the natural world. The focus of an empirical typology is on concrete characteristics amenable to reliable observation; it is heavily dependent on measurement and observation.[102] Therefore, a four-step measurement process is suggested to test the application of the postulated typology of police corruption. The four step process represents a triangulation methodology i.e. more than one independent measurement process.[103]

Step One—Definitions

In step one, field researchers must ascertain a specific police organization's professed normative definitions of various types of corrupt behavior and corrupt actors. Expectedly these corrupt behaviors and actors will be indentifiable through and by the categories and items of the typology. Police departments operate their own internal judicial systems which are in many ways independent of civil courts. Police officers, on and off duty, who break the law are not processed by the civil justice system unless the police choose to investigate and report it to civil authorities.[104] Most matters of police corruption are processed through departmental trials and procedures; therefore,

---

[102] See Theodore N. Ferdinand, *Typologies of Delinquency*, pp. 48-51.

[103] For a discussion of the triangulation measurement process see Eugene J. Webb and others, *Unobtrusive Measures: Nonreactive Research in the Social Sciences* (Chicago, 1966), p. 3.

[104] Bernard Cohen, *The Police Internal Administration of Justice* (New York, 1970), p. 1.

definitions found in the criminal justice system provide little information concerning police corruption.

Step one specifically requires (1) an examination and analysis of the written administrative rules and regulations of the department, including all orders (general, standing and special) and directives, (2) knowledge of the organizational structure and chain of command including provisions for internal security, (3) knowledge of formal and avowed standard operating procedures. Personal interviews of a cross section of the department's line, staff, administrative and support personnel are necessary to obtain data in categories (2) and (3).

Step Two—Police Justice System

Step two calls for an in-depth study of the department's stated methods and rationale in the labeling of behaviors and actors as corrupt i.e. the police justice system. Investigation areas include formal defining, screening, apprehending, exposing, adjudication, controlling and punishing procedures. This step will require a statistical analysis of all complaints lodged against police personnel for a specific time period. The source of complaint will be noted i.e. citizen, departmental, district attorney or court complaint. The procedures and rationale for processing and disposing of these specific complaints will be analyzed and recorded. Particular attention will be paid to the description of each complaint in order to make a comparative analysis with the formal definitions elicited in step one.

Step Three—Operating Informal Procedures

This step is designated to discover and analyze the operating informal procedures that determine (1) types of corrupt behavior and actors, (2) peer group support of corrupt behavior and actors, (3) organizational context of the various types of corrupt behaviors, and (4) actual departmental support.[105] In order to uncover these

---

[105] For an excellent treatment of a police department's internal judicial system and the difficulties posed by a police department's informal system of punishment see Bernard Cohen, *The Police Internal Administration of Justice in New York City.* For discussions of informal operating procedures within criminal justice systems see Egon Bittner, "The Police on Skid Row: A Study of Peace Keeping;" Jerome Skolnick, *Justice Without Trial;* David Sudnow, "Normal Crimes: Socio-

informal operating procedures, it is necessary to study police officers in their natural setting with as little interference as possible.[106] The most effective method available for the collection of data required for this step is participant observation by working police personnel.

Sociologists working as auxiliary or reserve police officers could observe police in their natural work setting, but this method has several disadvantages.[107] The auxiliary has limited access to department records and files. He is usually assigned with the more honest and trustworthy members of the police department; therefore, it is a matter of chance for him to observe corrupt behavior. The auxiliary is distrusted and disliked by most members of the police organization; consequently, he is excluded from conversations of police misconduct. These disadvantages apply, even more so, to any outsider who wishes to engage in the participant observation of the police.[108] Therefore, the authors suggest that research trained, cooperating police officers, *plants,* collect this data and exclusively report to members of the research team.

The use of disguised participant observers is viewed by some sociologists as a violation of professional ethics. Erickson states that it is unethical for a sociologist to misrepresent his identity and purpose

logical Features of the Penal Code in a Public Defenders Office," *Social Problems,* 32: 255-276 (Winter 1965).

[106] For discussions of the advantages of studying deviant behavior in its natural setting see Erving Goffman, *Relations in Public;* Jack D. Douglas, *American Social Order;* Ned Polsky, *Hustlers, Beats and Others* (Garden City, 1969), pp. 109-143; David Matza, *Becoming Deviant* (Englewood Cliffs, 1969); Aaron V. Cicourel, *The Social Organization of Juvenile Justice* (New York, 1968), pp. 1-22; Howard S. Becker, *Outsiders: Studies in the Sociology of Deviance,* pp. 166-176; Donald W. Ball, "Self and Identity in the Context of Deviance: The Case of Criminal Abortion," in Robert A. Scott and Jack D. Douglas (eds.): *Theoretical Perspectives on Deviance* (New York, 1972) pp. 158-186.

[107] Auxiliary, reserve or civilian police exist in a majority of cities over 10,000 population. These civilian police are selected, trained and controlled by the police organization. The auxiliary has authority only when on duty and is prohibited from making arrests off-duty. In a number of cities these civilian police officers work in the field with and under the supervision of experienced police officers. International City Managers Association, *Municipal Police Administration* 5th ed. (Chicago, 1961), pp. 423-424.

[108] A notable exception to this is the study by Reiss, but some of his research assistants were employed police officers. And even with police officers the only corruption they observed were types which arise opportunistically e.g. shakedowns and opportunistic theft. Albert J. Reiss, Jr., *The Police and the Public.*

and enter a domain to which he is not otherwise eligible.[109]   There are at least three reasons why this argument does not hold for participant observer police officers: (1) the use of police officers is the most effective field method available for the study of police corrupt behavior; (2) police officers are publicly accountable for their actions under research observations;[110] and (3) cooperating police officers (participant observers) observe behavior within their normal work milieu.   Only two facets of their work are disguised: (1) method of reporting and (2) purpose.

Research team members must be unknown to and exclusive from all members of the police organization.   Participant observation will cover the spatial and temporal occupational environments of working police personnel with particular attention to the interaction patterns observed in both routinized and problematic situations related to police corrupt behavior.   Setting, purpose, social behavior, frequency and duration of each police-citizen encounter will be recorded and analyzed.[111]   The reactions of all interactants including the police, the corruptors and other witnesses present in the interaction situation will be noted.[112]   Communication and action patterns of study include verbalizations, conversations, supportive interchanges, remedial interchanges, tiesigns, normal appearances, alien appearances, fronts, presentation of self, accounts, gestures, postures, demeanors, as well as decision making and action patterns.[113]   These encounters must be analyzed in terms of their immediate social contextual and trans-situational meanings.   Hopefully, this examination will partially explain the relation between rules (or situated uses of

---

[109] Kai T. Erickson, "A Comment on Disguised Observation in Sociology," *Social Problems, 14*: 366-372 (Spring, 1967).

[110] Lee Rainwater and David J. Pittman, "Ethical Problems in Studying a Politically Sensitive and Deviant Community," *Social Problems,* 14: 366 (Spring 1967).

[111] Claire Selltiz and others, *Research Methods in Social Relations* (Rev. Ed., New York, 1969), pp. 209-210. Encounters where the opportunity for corrupt behavior exists, but the officers demures or resists are important in the understanding of police corrupt behavior. Therefore, every police-citizen encounter must be analyzed.

[112] William J. Filstead, ed., "General Theoretical Framework: An Introduction," *An Introduction to Deviance* (Chicago, 1971).

[113] See Erving Goffman, *Relations in Public;* Marvin B. Scott and Stanford M. Lyman, "Accounts," *American Sociological Review, 302*: 46-62 (February 1968).

rules) and social action.[114] Moreover, this analysis will reveal the differentials and relationships among the organization's absolute norms, informal procedures, and situational rules that constitute the various types of police corruption.

Step Four—Actual Reactions

This step determines the police organization's operational definitions and reactions to different types of corrupt behavior i.e. corrupt behavior that has been observed by participant observation. Participant observers will use the normative definitions elicited by step one to identify corrupt behavior; this is necessary because this step ascertains actual police department reaction to behavior the police organization considers and defines as corrupt. Particular attention will be given to those acts which power structure members become cognizant of via personal observation, reports from other members of the police organization, reports from other criminal justice agencies and citizens complaints.[115] Participant observers will report to the research team the overt and covert reactions of the police organization to this observed behavior.

Data for analysis will include the nature of the act, interactants present, concrete setting, manner in which power structure members become aware of the act, identity of these power structure members, what is done with the information and the final action taken. The nature of the act encompasses the specific type of corrupt behavior, the professed rule or regulation violated, and the prescribed sanction for the act. The identity and reactions of corruptors, corrupted officers, witnesses (fellow officers, superior officers, citizens) present at the time of the act will be examined. The setting in which the corrupt behavior occurs will be analyzed since reactions may vary with the situation e.g. different reactions for street, business or court settings.

Police department reaction may be linked to the identity and manner in which power structure members become aware of the act and

---

[114] Jack D. Douglas, *American Social Order.*

[115] Power structure members of the police organization are those either in a position to initiate corrupt behavior investigations or those responsible for seeing that appropriate investigative agencies are informed of such behavior. Normally this will include all supervisory personnel, line, staff or administrative.

actors. Observers will note any differential application of sanctioning procedures; e.g. some supervisors may handle corrupt behavior informally and others may initiate formal investigations; certain subordinates may receive differential treatment. Formal or informal handling of acts of corruption may be contingent on the manner in which power structure members acquire knowledge of the act (e.g. personal observation, reports from police officers, citizens or other criminal justice agencies). Lastly, the final action (or lack of action) taken in each instance of observed corrupt behavior will be examined e.g. indifference, acceptance, condonation, administrative adjudication and disposition or criminal prosecution.

Hopefully, this step will reveal the patterns and differences (if any) between operational and normative definitions of corrupt behavior and the existence of any informal police justice systems which may determine actual departmental reaction to various types of corrupt behavior.

SUMMARY

The proposed typology and the triangulation methods suggested for testing purposes comprise the following elements: a series of common data bases, a reliable sampling model that recognizes interaction, a series of empirical indicators for each data base, and a series of testable conceptualizations.[116] The common data bases are overt corrupt behaviors operationally defined and identified in the typology. The study of this overt behavior through the use of professed normative definitions and actual departmental judicial procedures is insufficient to establish valid explanations of police corrupt behavior. Therefore, a reliable sampling model that recognizes interaction, the use of participant observers, is suggested. The empirical indicators for each data base are contained in five dimensions of study that include interactive and situational contingencies. Testable conceptualizations include (1) police corruption is best understood as organizational deviance and not as the exclusive behavior of individual officers; (2) police officers engage in certain types of corrupt practices in accordance with a temporization process among four sets of uncomplimentary norms, viz., formal and informal norms of the

---

[116] Norman K. Denzin, "Symbolic Interactionalism and Ethnomethodology: A Proposed Synthesis," *American Sociological Review*, 34: 925-926 (December 1969).

police organization, legal norms, and situational social meanings and rules; (3) there is not one but many analytical types of police corruption; (4) police corrupt behavior is a dynamic and progessive form of deviant behavior.

Future study guided by the proposed typology and the suggested methodology will hopefully empirically validate the conceptualizations proposed in this book. Moreover, future study should identify the programmatically intended formal structure of the police organization, the formal features that describe what is going on within the organization, and what unintended, unprogrammed and thus informal structures accompany this formal structure.[117]

---

[117] Egon Bittner, "The Concept of Organization," *Social Research,* 32: 239 (1965).

REFERENCES
Books

Ball, Donald W.: Self and Identity in the Context of Deivance: The Case of Criminal Abortion. In Scott, Robert A. and Douglas, Jack D. (Eds.): *Theoretical Perspectives on Deviance*. New York, Basic Books, 1972.

Becker, Howard S.: *Outsiders: Studies in the Sociology of Deviance*. New York, Free Press, 1963.

Bell, Daniel: *The End of Ideology*. New York, Free Press, 1960.

Block, Herbert A., and Geis, Gilbert: *Man Crime and Society: The Forms of Criminal Behavior*. New York, Random House, 1962.

Brannon, W. T.: *The Crooked Cops*. Chicago, Hall, 1962.

Chambliss, William J.: *Crime and the Legal Process*. New York, McGraw-Hill, 1969.

Cicourel, Aaron V.: *The Social Organization of Juvenile Justice*. New York, Wiley, 1968.

Citizens' Police Committee: *Chicago Police Problems*. Montclair, New Jersey: Patterson Smith Reprint, 1969. First published 1931.

Clinard, Marshall B., and Quinney, Richard: *Criminal Behavior Systems: A Typology*. New York, Holt, Rinehart, and Winston, 1967.

Cook, Fred J.: *The Corrupted Land: The Social Morality of Modern America*. New York, Macmillan, 1966.

Cressey, Donald R.: *Theft of the Nation*. New York, Harper and Row, 1969.

Cumming, Elaine, Cumming, Ian, and Edell, Laura: Policeman as Philosopher, Guide, and Friend. In Knudten, Richard D. (Ed.): *Crime, Criminology, and Contemporary Society*. Homewood, Dorsey, 1970.

Deutsch, Albert: *The Trouble with Cops*. Boston, Crown, 1955.

Dienstein, William: Sociology of Law Enforcement. In Knudten, Richard D. (Ed.): *Crime Criminology and Contemporary Society*. Homewood, Dorsey, 1971.

Douglas, Jack D.: *American Social Order*. New York, Free Press, 1971.

Edwards, George Judge: *The Police on the Urban Frontier: A Guide to Community Understanding*. New York, Institute of Human Relations, 1968.

Ferdinand, Theodore N.: *Typologies of Delinquency: A Critical Analysis*. New York, Random House, 1966.

Filstead, William J.: *An Introduction to Deviance*. Chicago, Markham, 1971.

Freeman, Howard E. and Jones, Wyatt C.: *Social Problems: Causes and Control*. Chicago, Rand McNally, 1970.

Gardiner, John A.: *The Politics of Corruption*. New York, Russell Sage Foundation, 1970.

Gibbons, Don C.: *Society, Crime, and Criminal Careers.* Englewood Cliffs, Prentice-Hall, 1968.

Gibbons, Don C.: *Changing the Lawbreaker. Englewood Cliffs,* Prentice-Hall, 1965.

Goffman, Erving: *Stigma: Notes on the Management of Spoiled Identity.* Englewood Cliffs, Prentice-Hall, 1963.

Goffman, Erving: *The Presentation of Self in Everyday Life.* Garden City, Doubleday, 1959.

Goffman, Erving: *Relations in Public.* New York, Basic Books, 1971.

Guenther, Anthony L.: *Criminal Behavior and Social Systems.* Chicago, Rand McNally, 1970.

Hahn, Harlan: *Police in Urban Society.* Beverly Hills, Sage, 1971.

Hempel, Carl G.: "Symposium: Problems of Concept and Theory Formation in the Social Sciences," *Science Language and Human Rights.* Vol. 1. Philadelphia Press, 1952, 65-80.

Johnson, Elmer H.: *Crime, Corrections, and Society.* Homewood, Dorsey, 1964.

Klein, Herbert T.: *The Police: Damned If They Do—Damned If They Don't.* New York, Crown, 1968.

Knudten, Richard D.: *Crime, Criminology, and Contemporary Soeicty.* Homewood, Dorsey, 1971.

Kobler, John: *Capone: The Life and World of Al Capone.* New York, Putnam's, 1971.

Korn, Richard R., and McCorkle, Lloyd W.: *Criminology and Penology.* New York, Holt, Rinehart, and Winston, 1959.

Lewis, Earl, and Blum, Richard H.: Selection Standards: A Critical Approach. In Blum, Richard H. (Ed.): *Police Selection.* Springfield, Thomas, 1964.

Matza, David: *Becoming Deviant.* Englewood Cliffs, Prentice-Hall, 1969.

McKelway, St. Clair: The Average Cop. In Sykes, Gresham M., and Drabeck, Thomas E. (Eds.): *Law and Lawless: A Reader in Criminology.* New York, Random, 1969.

McNamara, John H.: Uncertainties in Police Work: The Relevance of Police Recruits' Background and Training. In Bordua, David J. (Ed.): *The Police: Six Sociological Essays.* New York, Wiley, 1967.

Merton, Robert K.: *Social Theory and Social Structures.* New York, Free Press, 1958.

Messick, Hank: *Syndicate in the Sun.* New York, MacMillan, 1968.

Niederhoffer, Arthur: *Behind the Shield: The Police in Urban Society.* Anchor Books. Garden City, Doubleday, 1969.

Polsky, Ned: *Hustlers, Beats, and Others.* Anchor Books. Garden City, New York: Doubleday and Company, 1969.

Poston, Ted: The Numbers Racket. In Cressey, Donald R., and Ward, David A. (Eds.): *Delinquency, Crime, and Social Process.* New York, Harper and Row, 1960.

President's Commission on Law Enforcement and Administration of Justice. *Task Force Report: The Police.* Washington, D. C.: Government Printing Office.

Radano, Gene: *Walking the Beat: A New York Policeman Tells What It's Like on His Side of the Law.* Cleveland, World Pub., 1968.

Radzinowicz, Leon and Wolfgang, Marvin E.: *Crime and Justice, Vol. II. The Criminal in the Arms of the Law.* New York, Basic Books, 1971.

Reckless, Walter C.: *The Crime Problem.* 4th Ed. New York, Appleton, 1967.

Reiss, Albert J. Jr.: *The Police and the Public.* New Haven, Yale University Press, 1972.

Reiss, Albert J. Jr.: The Study of Deviant Behavior: Where the Action Is. In Lefton, Mark, Skipper, James K. Jr., and McGaghy, Charles H. (Eds.): *Approaches to Deviance.* New York, Appleton, 1968.

Reiss, Albert J. Jr., and Bordua, David J.: Environment and Organization: A Perspective on the Police. In Bordua, David J. (Ed.): *The Police: Six Sociological Essays.* New York, Wiley, 1967.

Rubington, Earl and Weinberg, Martin S.: *The Study of Social Problems.* New York, Oxford University Press, 1971.

Salerno, Ralph and Tompkins, John S.: *The Crime Federation.* Garden City, Doubleday, 1969.

Schur, Edwin M.: *Our Criminal Society: The Social and Legal Sources of Crime in America.* Englewood Cliffs, Prentice-Hall, 1969.

Schur, Edwin M.: *Crimes Without Victims—Deviant Behavior and Public Policy: Abortion, Homosexuality, Drug Addiction. Englewood Cliffs,* Prentice-Hall, 1965.

Selltiz, Claire, *et al.: Research Methods in Social Relations.* Revised One—Volume Edition. New York, Holt, Rinehart, and Winston, 1959.

Skolnick, Jerome H.: *Justice Without Trial: Law Enforcement in Democratic Society.* New York, Wiley, 1967.

Smith, Ralph Lee: *The Tarnished Badge.* New York, Crowell, 1965.

Sutherland, Edwin H.: The Fix. In Chambliss, William J. (Ed.): *Crime and the Legal Process.* New York, McGraw-Hill, 1969.

Sutherland, Edwin H. and Cressey, Donald R.: *Criminology.* 8th Ed. Philadelphia, Lippincott, 1970.

Sykes, Gresham M.: *Crime and Society.* New York, Random, 1967.

Tannenbaum, Frank: *Crime and the Community.* Boston, Ginn, 1938.

Tappan, Paul W.: *Crime, Justice, and Correction.* New York, McGraw-Hill, 1960.

The International City Managers' Association. *Municipal Police Administration.* 5th Ed. Chicago, International City Managers Association, 1961.

Turner, William W.: *The Police Establishment.* New York, Putnam's, 1968.

Tyler, Gus: *Organized Crime in America.* Ann Arbor, University of Michigan Press, 1969.

Webb, Eugene J. *et al.*: *Unobtrusive Measures: Non-Reactive Research in the Social Sciences.* Chicago, Rand-McNally, 1966.

Westley, William A.: *Violence and the Police: A Sociological Study of Law, Custom, and Morality.* Cambridge, M.I.T. Press, 1970.

Whyte, William F. Jr.: *Street Corner Society.* Chicago, University of Chicago Press. 1955.

Wilson, James Q.: *Varieties of Police Behavior.* New York, Antheneum, 1970.

Wilson, O. W.: *Police Administration.* 2nd Ed. New York, McGraw-Hill, 1963.

Winick, Charles and Kinsie, Paul M.: *The Lively Commerce: Prostitution in the United States.* Chicago, Quadrangle Books, 1971.

Journals

Bittner, Egon: The police on skid row: A study of peace keeping. *Am Sociol Rev. 32:* 699-715, 1967.

Bittner, Egon: The concept of organization. *Soc Res, 33:* 239-255, 1965.

Bordua, David J., and Reiss, Albert J. Jr.: Command control, and charisma: Reflections on police bureaucracy. *Am J Sociol, 72:* 68-76, 1966.

Buckley, Tom: Murphy among the meat eaters. *New York Times Magazine, 121:* 44-54, 1971.

Burnham, David: Graft here said to run into millions. *New York Times Magazine, CXIX, 119:* 1-18, 1970.

Burnham, David: How corruption is built into the system—and a few ideas for what to do about it. *New York,* pp. 30-37, September 21, 1970.

Cohen, Bernard: The police internal system of justice in New York City. *Journal of Criminal Law, Criminology, and Police Science, 63:* 54-68, 1972.

Cook, Fred J.: The pusher cop: The institutionalizing of police corruption. *New York,* pp. 22-30, August 16, 1971.

Denzin, Norman K.: Symbolic interactionism and ethnomethodology: A proposed synthesis. *Am Sociol Rev, 34:* 922-934, 1969.

Denzin, Norman K.: The logic of naturalistic inquiry. *Social Forces, 50:* 166-182, 1971.

Dougherty, Richard: The New York police. *Atlantic Monthly, 229:*6-10, 1972.

Erickson, Kai T.: A comment on distinguished observation in sociology. *Social Problems, 14:* 366-372, 1967.

Goldstein, Joseph: Police discretion not to invoke the criminal process: Low visibility decisions in the adminstration of criminal justice. *Yale Law Review, 69:* 543-544, 1960.

Hindelang, Michael J.: Bookies and Bookmaking: A Descriptive Analysis. *Crime and Delinquency, 17:* 245-255, 1971.

Ingersoll, John E.: The Police Scandal Syndrome. *Crime and Delinquency, 10:* 269-276, 1964.

Kemper, Theodore: Representative roles and legitimation of deviancy. *Social Problems, 13:* 288-298, 1966.

McIntyre, Jennie: Public attitudes toward crime and law enforcement. *Annals of the American Academy of Political and Social Sciences, 374:* 34-46, 1967.

Mitchell, Robert Edward: Organization as a key to police effectiveness. *Crime and Delinquency, 17*: 344-353, 1966.

Rainwater, Lee and Pittman, David J.: Ethical programs in studying a politically sensitive and deviant community. *Social Problems, 14*: 357-365, 1967.

Reiss, Albert J. Jr., and Black, Donald J.: Interrogation and the criminal process. *The Annals of the American Academy of Political and Social Sciences, 374*: 45-47, 1967.

Scott, Marvin B. and Lyman, Stanford M.: Accounts. *Am Sociol Rev., 33*: 46-62, 1968.

Stern, Mort: What makes a policeman go wrong? *Journal of Criminal Law, Criminology, and Police Science, 43*: 98-101, 1962.

Stoddard, Ellywn R.: The 'informal code' of police deviancy: A group approach to 'blue coat crime.' *Journal of Criminal Law, Criminology, and Police Science, 44*: 201-213, 1908.

Sudnow, David: Normal crimes: sociological features of the penal code in a public defender's office. *Social Problems, 32*: 255-276, 1965.

Wilson, O. W.: Police authority in a free society. *Journal of Criminal Law, Criminology, and Police Science, 54*: 175-177, 1963.

Miscellaneous

Bittner, Egon: *The Functions of the Police in Modern Society: A Review of Background Factors, Current Practices, and Possible Role Models.* U. S. Department of Health, Education, and Welfare, Publication No. (HSM) 72-9103.

Burnham, David: "Gamblers Links to Police Lead to Virtual Licensing," *New York Times,* CXIX, April 26, 1970, p. 1.

"Chicago Cops Under Fire," *Time* (July 10, 1973), 22.

Cohen, Bernard: *The Police Internal Administration of Justice in New York City.* New York, New York City, Rand Institute, November 1970.

Commission to Investigate Alleged Police Corruption. "Interim Report on Investigative Phase," 51 Chamber Street, New York, N. Y. (mimeographed)

"Cops on the Take," *Newsweek,* LXXVIII (November 1, 1971), 48-53.

Kefauver, Estes: *Third Interim Report of the Special Committee to Investigate Organized Crime in Gambling and Racketeering Activities.* Report No. 307. Government Printing Office, 1951.

"Police Use Own Words to Speak of Corruption," *New York Times,* CXIX, April 25, 1970, p. 18.

Wittels, David C. "Why Cops Turn Crooked," *Saturday Evening Post,* April 23, 1949, pp. 26-27, 104-107, 111, 114-122.

INDEX

NAME INDEX

B

Ball, Donald W., 45 fnt., 49
Becker, Howard S., 13 fnt., 45 fnt., 49
Bell, Daniel, 6 fnt., 49
Bittner, Egon, 3 fnt., 5 fnt., 11 fnt., 44 fnt., 49 fnt., 52-53
Black, Donald J., 11 fnt., 53
Bloch, Herbert A., 12 fnt., 49
Blum, Richard H., 5 fnt., 50
Bordua, David J., 8 fnt., 11-21 fnt., 19 fnt., 51-52
Brannon, W. T., 49
Buckley, Tom, 35 fnt., 52
Burnham, David, 23 fnt., 27 fnt., 30 fnt., 32 fnt., 37 fnt., 52-53

C

Chambliss, William J., 34 fnt., 49, 52
Cicourel, Aaron V., 45 fnt., 49
Clinard, Marshall B., 6 fnt., 49
Cohen, Bernard, 8 fnt., 43-44 fnt., 52-53
Cook, Fred J., 15 fnt., 17 fnt., 27-28 fnt., 30 fnt., 36 fnt., 49, 52
Cooper, Syndney, 35 fnt.
Cressey, Donald R., 5 fnt., 31-32 fnt., 49, 51-52
Cressey, F. R., 4 fnt.
Cumming, Elaine, 3 fnt., 49
Cumming, Ian, 3 fnt., 49

D

Denzin, Norman K., 10 fnt., 48 fnt., 52
Deutsch, Albert, 4 fnt., 13, 22 fnt., 24-25 fnt., 49
Dienstein, William, 3 fnt., 50
Dougherty, Richard, 16 fnt., 27 fnt., 33 fnt., 52
Douglas, Jack D., 9 fnt., 24 fnt.,
Drabeck, Thomas E., 23 fnt., 50

E

Edell, Laura, 3 fnt., 49
Edwards, George Judge, 50
Rickson, Kai T., 45-46 fnt., 53

F

Ferdinand, Theodore N., 6 fnt., 43 fnt., 50
Filstead, William J., 46 fnt., 50 45 fnt., 47 fnt., 49-50
Fisch, Joseph, 15 fnt.
Freeman, Howard E., 31 fnt., 50
Freeman, Lucy, 29 fnt.

G

Gardiner, John A., 5 fnt., 31 fnt., 33 fnt., 50
Geiss, Gilbert, 12 fnt., 49
Gibbons, Don C., 5-6 fnt., 50
Goffman, Erving, 9 fnt., 14 fnt., 28 fnt., 45-46 fnt., 50
Goldstein, Joseph, 8 fnt., 53
Guenther, Anthony L., 4 fnt., 50

H

Hahn, Harlan, 12 fnt., 50
Hempel, Carl H., 6 fnt., 50
Hindelang, Michael J., 28 fnt., 53
Hughes, Harold, 30 fnt.

I

Ingersoll, John E., 6 fnt., 53

J

Javits, Jacob A., 30 fnt.
Johnson, Elmer H., 5 fnt., 50
Jones, Wyatt C., 31 fnt., 50